THE BOSWELLIAN HERO

THE BOSWELLIAN HERO

by

WILLIAM C. DOWLING

Athens
THE UNIVERSITY OF GEORGIA
PRESS

Set in 11 on 14 point Janson type
Printed in the United States of America

Library of Congress Cataloging in Publication Data

Dowling, William C
  The Boswellian hero.

  Includes bibliographical references and index.

  1. Boswell, James, 1740–1795—Criticism and interpretation. 2. Johnson, Samuel, 1709–1784, in
fiction, drama, poetry, etc. I. Title.

PR3325.D6 1979   828'.6'09   78–5885
            ISBN 0–8203–0461–1

Material in the Preface, Introduction, and Chapter
3 previously appeared in Harvard English Studies,
vol. 8 (copyright © 1978 by the President and
Fellows of Harvard College), and in *Studies in
Scottish Literature*, vol. 10 (October 1972). Grate-
ful acknowledgment is given to the editors of each
volume for permission to reproduce the material.

FOR WALTER JACKSON BATE

CONTENTS

PREFACE

SOME YEARS AGO, in the course of a general discussion of symbolic meaning, Ernst Cassirer referred to the literary work as a "self-contained cosmos with its own center of gravity." The phrase may be taken to express an axiom of modern criticism, the notion that life and literature, whatever else we may find to say about them, represent entirely separate realities. At the same time, as a metaphor giving expression to a powerful intuitive conviction, the phrase calls to mind a stage in modern theory when the notion of literary autonomy was still a matter of considerable controversy. In the ordinary course of things one might suppose the controversy long since laid to rest—no axiom, perhaps, is without its troubled history—and feel free to turn to the work of the moment. When the work occupying the moment is literary interpretation of three major biographical narratives written by James Boswell, however, one soon discovers that one has managed to wander well out of the ordinary course of things.

Any literary consideration of Boswell raises certain questions about biography as a genre, and behind these questions may be glimpsed the larger problem of our usual distinction between fiction and nonfiction. A reader equally interested in biography and theory will come to see the debates of the recent past in a curious light: what is usually assumed to have been a straightforward advance in the theory of interpretation now appears as a more complicated maneuver designed to avoid, in the interests of general strategy, the positions so formidably occupied by biography and factual narrative generally. To view *Tom Jones* and *Hamlet* and *Paradise Lost* as self-contained worlds of motive and action is now both comfortable and orthodox. To approach the *Life of Johnson* or *The Decline and Fall of the Roman Empire* in the same way is neither.

The emergence of modern critical theory provides a background against which our normal distinction between factual and imaginative literature appears as something of an anomaly, and it is when we attempt to explain the anomaly that Boswell assumes a special importance, for the history of Boswell criticism in the modern period is in one sense the history of a general effort to come to terms with a categoric distinction going back at least as far as Aristotle. In preferring poetry to history in the *Poetics*, with the secondary implication that the real and the imaginary present antagonistic claims, Aristotle was taking for granted something that only now begins to appear in the light of a dilemma, and the reluctance of a modern critic to approach the *Life of Johnson* as he would approach *King Lear* or *Paradise Lost* may be explained in Aristotelian terms: behind the *Life*, he feels, lurks the presence of a "real" Samuel Johnson who, because he once existed in historical reality, does not belong entirely to the world of the literary imagination.

The question of whether the *Life of Johnson* may be approached as a literary work is in this context a question whether Johnson as he exists in the pages of the *Life* is a hero in the sense that Hamlet and Lear are heroes, one whom we must dissociate from the historical Johnson in much the same way as we dissociate Shakespeare's Richard II from Richard II of England. From a purely theoretical viewpoint the same question may be put in broader terms, not as a question whether the two Johnsons do not in some sense correspond but whether a certain type of meaning in the *Life*, a meaning we usually consider valuable and worthwhile, becomes accessible only when we make some such distinction. Such questions reveal the precise sense in which our normal conception of biography stands in an anomalous relation to modern criticism generally.

At the same time, as the very terms in which we pose them suggest, modern theory has provided answers to questions like these. Even to speak of "two Johnsons," we will be told by the theorist, is to speak of two imaginary beings who exist on precisely the same plane of ideal reality. The argument here is a familiar one: the process through which one comes to know Boswell's Johnson is the process through which one comes to know any literary protagonist, from Odysseus to Leopold Bloom. Yet the "real" Johnson, though the process through which one comes to know him is somewhat different, is scarcely more substantial a creature and when analyzed closely dissolves into the scattered evidence from which he has been constructed—Piozzi or Hawkins or Burney, letters or writings or gleanings, a voice heard in the *Rambler* or *Rasselas,* a visit during some scholarly holiday to the house in Gough Square.

From this perspective, literature and the version of reality we call "history" are equally provisional, and any defense of the distinction between factual and imaginative literature assumes the uncomfortable burden of showing why we should discriminate against one in the name of the other. Again we are dealing with a familiar theoretical argument, that to approach the *Life of Johnson* as literature is simply to regard it as belonging to a special realm of provisional reality, one created solely out of language. At the level of the individual work and at the level of relations among works—for example among the *Life,* the *Tour to the Hebrides,* and the *Tour to Corsica*—this is a complete and autonomous realm, and if its truth is a provisional truth, so perhaps is any other. To speak of Boswell as narrator and Johnson as hero, to speak of Reynolds and Burke and Goldsmith as characters in a biographical story—all this is only to announce a concern for *literary* truth.

Modern criticism of Boswell, and of biography as a genre, has never really come to terms with this argument, for theory is only an embarrassment when we assume an essential antagonism between the factual and the imaginative. Yet there has been some uneasiness among critics of biography, and a tentative compromise: Aristotle's categories have disappeared to reemerge as what criticism now calls correspondence and coherence, correspondence being the relation of a written work to the world of historical fact, coherence the symbolic principle we recognize when we talk about its "meaning." Might not criticism, it has been asked, take the comfortable view that coherence is simply something a good biography manages to achieve even while it is giving us dates and names and places, something which leaves the impress of the artistic imagination on a lifeless mass of factual material? Such a view, if it were reasonable, would seem to avoid most of the problems raised by the old antagonism of art and history by taking biography as a kind of synthesis of the two.

Unfortunately this view merely preserves that antagonism in disguise, for under the names of coherence and correspondence we are still dealing with the concepts of the literary and the unliterary. This is why Boswell's role as a reporter of events has remained to trouble modern criticism, for whenever we make claims for Boswell's literary artistry by protesting that he was "more than" a reporter, we reveal a certain hidden assumption: the more "artistic" or "imaginative" Boswell was, the less will he appear as a mere transcriber of facts, a mere reporter. But then the contrary is true also: the more "objective" Boswell was, the more assiduous and accurate in getting down on paper what he actually saw and heard, the less will he appear artistic or imaginative. This, pushed to an extreme, would be to take the *Life of Johnson* as pure record, what we would get if we had been able to set a tape recorder in the corner of the drawing room at Bolt Court or Streatham.

This is in fact the way the nineteenth century looked at the *Life of Johnson* and at Boswell as its creator. The twentieth-century reaction, and the beginning of the compromise with modern theory, may be dated from the discovery of the Mala-

hide papers, which for the first time provided scholars with the
actual materials Boswell used in writing the *Life of Johnson*,
among them the notes from which he recreated Johnson's conversation. Geoffrey Scott, the first editor of the Malahide papers,
undertook the conclusive refutation of the Boswell-as-stenogra-
pher view, basing his argument on an appeal to these notes: *"they
are not written during the conversation, but . . . when he gets
home, at the end of the day, or the next day."*[1] Since the appearance of the Isham edition of the papers, Scott's argument has
been repeated in virtually every piece of commentary on Boswell that could accommodate its reiteration, often with a barely
disguised air of triumph.

Scott's discovery was a momentous event in Boswell scholarship, and only the most careful survey of subsequent writing on
Boswell will reveal the process through which his argument was
gradually made to assume a burden of implication it was never
meant to bear. For a time a way out of the larger impasse seemed
clear: though we do not often let simple information about an
author's habits of composition alter our total perception of his
works, Boswell transported by the magic of new evidence from
the drawing room to his study was now taken as the very symbol
of the biographer as artist. Boswell in his study, in dressing gown
and slippers and working from notes, was selecting and recalling
rather than merely reporting: "Boswell generally knows his story
something as a novelist does. . . . It would be naive to suppose
that his knowledge of subsequent events is not affecting his writing. It helps him to select his details meaningfully, to create a
significant forward-straining tension."[2]

From tape recorder, in other words, to artist manqué. This is
the approach that has dominated Boswell criticism in recent
years, one that is represented at its most intelligent in W. K.
Wimsatt's essay "The Fact Imagined." Wimsatt focuses on Boswell's selection of detail, in which he sees something not so very
different from what we normally think of as the creative process:

because life as Boswell experienced it was reconstituted in Boswell's imagination before he wrote, and because the imaginative act always lies behind the act of writing, we can trace in his narratives the transforming impulse that makes life into art. If we are to claim Boswell's works as literature, we will find our justification "in the subtle ranges and conflicts which he manages, in his firmness of detail and purity of verbal style—in his general artistry as a journalist."[3] The solution is not unattractive, and only from the viewpoint of interpretive logic are we likely to notice that it leaves the question of correspondence unresolved: we are still talking about the way Boswell handled "real" experience.

If we take the path of recent Boswell criticism, we thus begin with something like the nineteenth-century notion of the *Life of Johnson* as pure biographical record, but we immediately add that "it is more than a biographical record, that it is a work of art."[4] The dilemma here is unhappily obvious: as long as we are assuming some crucial relationship between the *Life* and "objective" reality, all we can do is keep showing in newer and more ingenious ways that although Boswell was a reporter, he was in some mysterious sense "more than" a reporter. In a recent significant essay on Boswell and the problem of biography, Ralph W. Rader pursues this logic to its end, which is a purely affectivist posture. Rader does not argue for anything quite so simple as a je ne sais quoi that allows certain works of history and biography to qualify as literature, but some such view lies behind his observations on Boswell and Gibbon. Both the *Life of Johnson* and the *Decline and Fall* are works that have somehow "transcended" an unliterary category: "such works become literature by transcending while fulfilling the usual purpose of history and biography, to provide true knowledge of the human past."[5]

In what follows I should like to explore an alternative way out of this dilemma, one suggested by the theoretical arguments earlier presented in summary form. For art and history, coherence and correspondence, have from the viewpoint of modern theory been placed in false conflict: they are not qualities of biography but aspects in which biography can be seen, in much the same way as we can look at a Greek vase both as an expression of man's visual imagination and as a thing for carrying water. The consequences are obvious: to read the *Life of Johnson* as literature is only to begin where all criticism must begin, with an awareness of its self-contained nature as a work of art—something that is in no way inconsistent with its being simultaneously a repository of facts about the "real" Samuel Johnson. If one discovers, as Strabo did, that Homer tells us a good deal about the geography of the ancient Mediterranean, that does not make the *Iliad* and the *Odyssey* chiefly valuable as geography texts.

The central insight of modern theory, perhaps, is that literary autonomy derives from the more basic principle that there is nothing inherent in any written work which makes it a priori literature or not literature, that this happens only with our decision to ask a certain kind of question about it (why do Anglo-Saxon dragons guard ancient treasures? why is the ghost in Elsinore?) and to suspend others (do dragons exist? are there ghosts?). This is not to exclude other kinds of inquiry: a geographer may still want to ask about Homer's geographical accuracy, a Johnson scholar about the dependability of Boswell's sources, and so on. But such questions are no longer assumed to be literary questions.

One solution to the problem of biography therefore lies in an awareness that it is the reader who approaches any work as literature—the individual reader, not polite readers or learned readers or the community of readers. The *Life of Johnson* is not a literary work because it has managed to transcend an unliterary category but becomes a literary work at precisely the moment we begin to ask about the meaning of Johnson's melancholy in the same spirit as we ask about Lear's madness or Hamlet's indecision. At that moment we are seeing Boswell's biographical story as an image of life, a representation of general nature, and this is something we are entitled to do with any work. From a Jeremy Taylor sermon to *The Voyage of the Beagle*, anything in language becomes literature if it seems to one reader worth the effort to consider its literary meaning. Biography, representing a rich and complex narrative tradition extending from before Plutarch to the present, is perhaps well worth the effort.

This essay gained much from my discussions with Michael Rewa when I was a Senior Fellow at Dartmouth College. In the intervening years I have received important advice and encouragement from a number of friends and fellow-scholars—John Gordon, Linda Dowling, Ilona and Robert Bell, R. A. Lanham, Morton Bloomfield—and I thank them. My debt to two colleagues in the eighteenth century—Frank Brady and Walter Jackson Bate—is too large to be acknowledged and can only be mentioned.

THE BOSWELLIAN HERO

INTRODUCTION

THE TWENTIETH CENTURY thinks of James Boswell as a dia-
rist, a writer whose major subject, pursued indefatigably through
the thousands of pages of his private journal, was his own life.
Boswell's great biography of Johnson is of course still regarded
as his finest achievement, but since the recovery of his journal
even that has been seen in a new light: "the *Life of Johnson*, in
the years when Boswell knew him, is essentially a part of this
journal. . . . The Johnson-record flows in and out of the personal
Boswell-record and is not different in kind. The vast, bracing
difference is the subject matter."[1] Almost inevitably such an observation suggests an almost purely autobiographical way of
reading the *Life of Johnson*, with an inevitable result: the reader
begins to see the Johnson of the *Life* only as another of the innumerable cast of characters who populate Boswell's vast journal; as an inhabitant, that is, of Boswell's world.

But the *Life of Johnson* is only incidentally an exercise in Boswellian autobiography. Boswell is present during a good deal of
the story, of course, for he is as much a character in it as Burke or
Reynolds or Goldsmith, but it is always clear to us that the young
man who comes down to London from Edinburgh in his twenty-
second year, and whose annual pilgrimage to the metropolis becomes a regular feature of his later life, has entered a world that
revolves around Johnson, that is dominated by Johnson, that in
some essential respects may even be said to be identified with
Johnson. It seems just as obvious that Boswell's conception of his
own work sprang from a certain high notion of Johnson as a
public character and that the impulse behind the *Life* is the very

opposite of the private or autobiographical. "However inferior in nature," Boswell observes at one point, the *Life of Johnson* "may in one respect be assimilated to the ODYSSEY. Amidst a thousand entertaining and instructive episodes the HERO is never long out of sight . . . and HE, in the whole course of the history, is exhibited by the Authour for the best advantage of his readers" (I.12).[2] Such a remark suggests, if nothing else, a concern with the hero as a public figure.

When we consider the *Life of Johnson* along with the two other major narratives Boswell published during his lifetime, the comparison with Homeric epic suggests a good deal more. The *Tour to Corsica*, which is the story of Boswell's encounter with the Corsican leader Pascal Paoli, and the *Tour to the Hebrides*, which is the story of his Highland journey with Johnson in 1773, are usually classified as travel books, but both are really books about heroes, men who represent what Carlyle called "superior natures" and whose moral nature Boswell found a matter of considerable fascination. When the three narratives are taken together a more significant conclusion begins to emerge: behind Boswell's portrayal of Paoli and his two portrayals of Johnson there lies a single conception of the heroic character, one which reaches beyond the particular narrative situation to a final vision of man's dilemma in the modern world. It is this conception I have in mind when I speak of "the Boswellian hero," as one speaks of "the Byronic hero," meaning not Manfred or Don Juan or Childe Harold specifically, but the idea of anguished and alienated humanity that lies behind all three.

Boswell's great subject is the hero in an unheroic world. To speak of the Boswellian hero is really to speak of a certain dramatic situation that is explored in a different way in each of his three narratives, one which takes the simple figure of the hero as the symbolic focus of larger and more complex moral concerns. We get a clue to this situation in the now commonplace observation that the Samuel Johnson of the *Life* and the *Tour to the*

Hebrides seems at times like a seventeenth-century being, someone living spiritually in the age of Milton, Hobbes, and Browne
and existing only uncomfortably in the intellectual climate of
the eighteenth century. A similar suggestion lies behind the comparison, so obvious to most contemporary readers of the *Tour
to Corsica*, between Paoli and the heroes of Plutarch's *Lives*. But
the idea of the hero as a man living out of his time is only the beginning of Boswell's theme, for in developing a complicated appeal to the conventions of heroic literature and to a certain myth
of the heroic past, each of his narratives also dramatizes the character of an age that has placed men like Johnson and Paoli in
spiritual isolation.

The hero in a world where heroism is possible exists within a
community of shared belief, for his personality and his actions
always give expression to certain values which, taken together,
sustain the society from which he has emerged. His role is thus
ultimately symbolic, which is why we usually think of the hero
as a literary rather than a social or historical figure. As Northrop
Frye has observed, the hero in this situation is a leader: "he has
authority, passions, and powers of expression far greater than
ours, but what he does is subject both to social criticism and to
the order of nature. This is the hero of the *high mimetic* mode,
of most epic and tragedy, and is primarily the kind of hero Aristotle had in mind."[3] But while social criticism of the hero may
form the actual subject of epic and tragedy, as when we find
Achilles sulking in his tent or Antony abandoning the concerns
of empire for Cleopatra, the idea of a dynamic relationship between the hero and a unified society is always retained. When
Aristotle said that Homer makes men better than they are,
Thomas Edwards explains, he did not mean better ethically or
morally, "but in their fuller representation of capacities that in
other men remain undeveloped, unexpressed—in short, more
potent."[4]

In the epic, perhaps because it is the earliest literary form, we see the relationship between the hero and society as a paradigm of unified concern (tragedy, on the other hand, is usually about the breakdown of this relationship). But while in the epic "the preservation of an ordered society is the highest good and the goal towards which the hero's physical and intellectual discipline is bent,"[5] it is also true that the society has in an important sense created the hero. In defending his society against monsters or foreign enemies, or in leading his companions to a new city or back to an ancestral home, the epic hero symbolizes the idea of human potentiality open to any man who exists in a community of shared conviction, for "so long as one lives within an accepted structure of belief and value, he follows customary lines without raising fundamental questions, and human energy flows unimpeded into activity."[6] Heroic literature dramatizes an idea of individual freedom arising from social coherence, and it is this, as much as its portrayal of great actions, that appeals to the imagination of ordinary men.

When a society feels itself to be disintegrating, there is thus a nostalgia for heroes that is also a nostalgia for the community of shared belief. When we see Matthew Arnold, for instance, excluding *Empedocles* from his collected poems because it pictures a situation in which "suffering finds no vent in action; in which a continuous state of mental distress is prolonged, unrelieved by incident, hope, or resistance; in which there is everything to be endured, nothing to be done" or urging modern poets to form their imaginations on "the great works of Homer, Aeschylus, and Virgil," to choose as their subject "some noble action of a heroic time," we are seeing a longing for that symbolic union of individual and society he has found in ancient literature. A similar nostalgia lies behind John Stuart Mill's plaintive wish that modern education would imitate the simpler pedagogy of a time when old romances "filled the youthful imagination with pictures of heroic men," which is really a wish that modern society could recreate itself (with due concessions to change) in the image of the heroic age.

In its purest form this nostalgia for the heroic past is a late nineteenth-century development, one which followed the decline of the romantic myth of the free self and lasted until existential thought gave a new form to questions about the relationship between self and society. During this period, even when the hero is left out of the picture, we see a continuing nostalgia for the spiritually coherent world that was assumed to have produced him. "If the London merchants of our day competed together in writing lyrics," laments Yeats in his *Autobiography*, "they would not, like the Tudor merchants, dance in the open street before the house of the victor; nor do the great ladies of London finish their balls on the pavement before their doors as did the great Venetian ladies, even in the eighteenth century, conscious of an all-enfolding sympathy." This is the other side of Yeats's obsession with heroic myth, with Cuchulain and Oisin and the rest, and even of his half-tragic hope, as an Irish nationalist, that Irish art could once again create a world in which hero and bard and peasant were at one.

At a certain point we see this nostalgia, which began by finding in heroic literature a symbolic refuge from modern anxiety, being transformed into an actual myth of the heroic past. Though the beginnings of the myth go back to the Renaissance—it is ultimately a response to the dilemma introduced by the Renaissance idea of the individual as a separate force in society—it is again something which attains its most characteristic form in the nineteenth century. Like all myths it uses an imaginary past to explain an otherwise confusing present: the notion that the possibilities of heroic action were actually greater in the primitive villages of ancient Greece or Scandinavia than in post-Romantic England is one that never needs to be proved objectively, for it does not arise to fulfill the demands of objective truth. The theme is one we see again and again, for instance, in the novels of George Eliot, where the disembodied idealism of a major character conflicts tragically with the unheroic reality of the present age. "A new Theresa will hardly have the opportunity for reforming a conventual life," says Eliot at the end of *Middlemarch*, "any more than a new Antigone will spend her heroic piety in daring all for the sake of a brother's burial: the medium in which their ardent deeds took shape is for ever gone."

The myth is ultimately one of decline, the spiritual decline that was supposed to have accompanied material progress, and it seized upon the hero mainly as the symbol of a lost potentiality for noble action. Thus Carlyle, in a series of lectures about great men, feels compelled to begin with an indictment of his own time: "this, for reasons which it will be worth while some time to inquire into, is an age that as it were denies the existence of great men; denies the desirableness of great men." Carlyle's lecture on Johnson in *Heroes and Hero-Worship* is a typically eccentric product of his eccentric genius, but it is indirectly a brilliant commentary on one of the major themes of Boswellian narrative. For Carlyle came to Johnson through Boswell, and the lecture in *Heroes* is really about the Johnson he discovered in the pages of the *Life*. No one since has perceived so clearly the fatal disparity between Johnson's character and that of his age: "The Eighteenth was a *Sceptical* Century; in which little word there is a whole Pandora's Box of miseries. Scepticism means not intellectual Doubt alone, but moral Doubt; all sorts of infidelity, insincerity, spiritual paralysis. Perhaps, in few centuries that one could specify since the world began, was a life of Heroism more difficult for a man. That was not an age of Faith,—an age of Heroes! The very possibility of Heroism had been, as it were, formally abnegated in the minds of all. Heroism was gone for ever; Triviality, Formulism and Commonplace were come for ever."

In place of retrospective denunciation Boswell gives us a fully dramatized picture of the unheroic present, but his judgment of the eighteenth century involves a similar dismay. The world Boswell describes is one in which intellectual doubt seems to have changed suddenly and mysteriously into moral doubt and where spiritual paralysis has become the price of that noble scepticism which was to have set men free. The picture is bleak, and it embodies a profoundly conservative response to the invisible forces of what we now call Enlightenment rationalism, for if some took this as the time when Reason, in Wordsworth's phrase, seemed intent on making of herself a prime enchantress, it was left to others to see the enchantment in its evil aspect. Boswell was one of these, and his vision of the age tends to isolate the later eighteenth century as the time of spiritual crisis and to view men like Johnson and Paoli as figures imprisoned by the age. "I have lived," Johnson would say in the *Life*, "to see things all as bad as they can be."

Boswell's portrayal of the later eighteenth century tends to make the age into a kind of anti-Enlightenment, from which the only refuge is the memory of a nobler past. This is not quite the myth of the heroic past I have spoken of previously, for it arises less from romantic nostalgia than from a sense of present crisis; but it is a related idea, and resembles the nearer past Burke appeals to as a witness against his own barbarously "rational" age: "men were not then quite shrunk from their natural dimensions by a degrading and sordid philosophy, and fitted for low and vulgar deceptions. . . . This was reserved to our time, to quench the little glimmerings of reason which might break in upon the solid darkness of this enlightened age." Under the name of philosophy, of course, Burke is referring to the deified Reason of the French Revolution, just as Boswell is when he speaks in the *Life* of "that detestable sophistry which has been lately imported from France, under the false name of Philosophy, and with a malignant industry has been employed against the peace, good order, and happiness of society" (I.11–12). But the goddess Reason is only the final symbol of the forces that have made the age a time of invisible strife.

When Burke speaks of men being shrunk from their natural dimensions, he is perhaps to be suspected of partisan eloquence, for we do not look for an evenhanded estimate of the present age in his *Reflections on the Revolution in France*. Yet it is precisely there that we discern the beginnings of that disenchantment with Enlightenment rationalism which became Carlyle's theme and which was later to turn into a general anxiety about the fate of the genuine individual in modern society. By the middle of the nineteenth century the issue is no longer partisan; it has become a defining characteristic of the time, and usually takes the form of an epitaph for greatness: the age, as Newman says, has become "the paradise of little men, and the purgatory of great ones." Though it took nearly a century for the problem to emerge in so general and dramatic a form, this is the major theme of Boswellian narrative. Like Burke's *Reflections*, Boswell's works stand at the very beginning of a period of moral doubt that has not ended today.

For just this reason, it is often illuminating to look back at Boswellian narrative through the medium of nineteenth-century moral anxiety, for Boswell made the hero's life a drama of what the nineteenth century saw as its own dilemma: "those who dwell in the tower of ancient faiths look about them in constant apprehension, misgiving, and wonder, with the hurried uneasy mien of people living amid earthquakes. The air seems full of missiles, and all is doubt, hesitation, and shivering expectancy."[7] Only in the *Life of Johnson*, perhaps, is the sense of present crisis this pronounced, but the metaphor gives us the essential situation of the hero in the *Tour to Corsica* and the *Tour to the Hebrides*, where Paoli and Johnson appear as men dwelling within the towers of their separate faiths. For spiritual survival in an unheroic age inevitably involves making a kind of moral sanctuary of the past, and an isolated structure of personal values takes the place of that community of shared conviction that sustained the great men of earlier times. But the concept brings with it an artistic problem—only the dreamer takes total refuge in the past, and Johnson and Paoli are both profoundly involved with the present. How, then, to turn the simple contrast between man and age into a drama of engagement, one which will show the hero, only half-conscious of his own greatness, living in a time that denies the desirableness of great men?

Boswell's answer was to present the tension between the man and his age as a *generic* tension; that is, continuously to associate Johnson and Paoli with the high protagonists of heroic literature and to associate their milieus with the lower worlds of the lesser literary modes (specifically, pastoral, romance, and comic novel). In Boswellian narrative the concept of higher and lower genres—similar to the one we find, for instance, in Warton's *Essay on Pope*—is converted into an internal dramatic principle. This is the principle of tension we often see at work in comic literature, as when Don Quixote rides forth full of heroic aspirations into the everyday world of sixteenth-century Spain, or Fielding describes a squabble among provincial women in Homeric language, but in Boswell it becomes a highly serious metaphor for the moral isolation of an actual great man. Though the statement demands a good deal of elaboration, we do not go far wrong if we perceive Johnson and Paoli as high mimetic heroes existing in low mimetic worlds.

We see this association of the hero with a symbolic past in its simplest form in the *Tour to Corsica*. The *Tour* ends with Pitt's remark that Paoli is "one of those men who are no longer to be found but in the *Lives* of Plutarch"—a remark which takes on its full significance only when we realize that Pitt knew Paoli only through Boswell's description. For when it concerns Paoli, the *Tour* is a continuous invocation of the heroic past, one that can invest the most commonplace incident with associative meaning: "having dogs for his attendants is another circumstance about Paoli similar to the heroes of antiquity. Homer represents Telemachus so attended: δύω κύνες ἀργοὶ ἕποντο. But the description given of the family of Patroclus applies better to Paoli: ἐννέα τῷ γε ἄνακτι τραπεζῆες κύνες ἦσαν" (197). Or one that, in more direct circumstances, can move to a dramatic revelation of Paoli's actual immersion in the heroic past, as when he spontaneously gives a catalogue raisonné of ancient heroes: "his characters of them were concise, nervous, and just. I regret that the fire with which he spoke on such occasions so dazzled me that I could not recollect his sayings so as to write them down when I retired from his presence. He just lives in the times of antiquity" (191).

The *Tour to Corsica* gives us, in short, a hero who seems to have stepped out of the pages of Plutarch or Livy into the unheroic world of eighteenth-century Corsica. For Paoli's island dominion contains only the simplest of agricultural communities, sparsely populated and in large measure isolated from the outside world. Yet Boswell finds in this isolation another kind of significance, and his portrayal of Corsican society moves always toward that myth of an irrecoverable Golden Age we discover in Virgil or Theocritus. Again, the associative process ranges from trivial incidents—"we lay down by the side of the first brook, put our mouths to the stream and drank sufficiently. It was just being for a little while one of the 'prisca gens mortalium' who ran about in the woods eating acorns and drinking water" (168–69)—to more elaborate evocations of the pastoral ideal of virtuous simplicity and peace: "these fathers have a good vineyard and an excellent garden. They have between thirty and forty beehives in long wooden cases or trunks of trees. . . . When they want honey they burn a little juniper-wood, the smoke of which makes the bees retire. . . . By taking the honey in this way they never kill a bee. They seemed much at their ease, living in peace and plenty" (165).

The tension between hero and milieu in the *Tour* is a simple one. Like the heroic age, the pastoral world is a fiction invented by poets, one which looks backward to a situation more mythic than real, and Paoli and his people appear in Boswell's book as figures separated by both time and geography from the complicated modernity of eighteenth-century Europe. If Paoli is isolated from his society, living imaginatively in the times of antiquity and forming his mind to a glory unattainable since the days of Homer, the isolation is not a tragic one. For Boswell makes Paoli a symbol simply of unfulfilled greatness, a quality of mind and character which, denied expression in heroic action, can express itself only in the mystery of personality. The theme is developed more elaborately in his books about Johnson, but not until the *Life*, where disparity between hero and society is so radical as to become a metaphor of spiritual isolation, do its tragic implications emerge. Paoli, the Plutarchan spirit living in a separate pastoral world, is the simplest incarnation of the Boswellian hero.

In the *Tour to the Hebrides* the theme of the isolated hero is complicated by the journey motif of the narrative, for it is not Johnson's society that provides the setting but the primitive world of the Scottish Highlands, where "simplicity and wildness, and all the circumstances of a remote time or place" greet a traveler from the modern age. As in the *Life*, Boswell often identifies Johnson with London, but here the identification has a different significance, for London in the *Life* is a symbol of the busy, complicated, modern world, and the immediate theater of Johnson's painful personal drama. In the *Tour*, from the time when Boswell first wonders if he can get Johnson to abandon "the felicity of a London life," to the time when he rejoices that the journey has actually come to pass—"as I have always been accustomed to view him as a permanent London object, it would not be much more wonderful to me to see St. Paul's church moving along where we now are" (V.347)—we see that symbolic London receding into the distance and the forgotten society and wild landscape of the Hebrides becoming a present reality. Johnson's Highland tour is metaphorically a journey into the past.

As a traveler Johnson has thus escaped the conflict between self and society that underlies his personal struggle in the *Life*, and Boswell's emphasis falls instead on that mysterious quality of mind that makes him a great man. For in leaving London Johnson has also left behind his fame as a philosopher and moralist, and during the journey we see him recreating in actual life the magisterial persona of the *Rambler* or *Rasselas*. It is in this light that we should take the epigraph from *Baker's Chronicle* which Boswell places at the beginning of his narrative—"he was of an admirable pregnancy of wit, and that pregnancy much improved by continual study from his childhood; by which he had gotten such a promptness in expressing his mind, that his extemporal speeches were little inferior to his premeditated writings"—for it is through conversation that Johnson continuously reveals the greatness of his moral vision, until, by the end of the *Tour*, we have come to assent to Boswell's portrayal of his hero as one "whose powers of mind were so extraordinary, that ages may revolve before such a man shall again appear" (V.416).

In the *Tour* the association of the hero with a symbolic past becomes a matter of imaginative response, as when, for instance, we see Johnson discovering in a decayed Highland cathedral the memory of a lost medieval Christianity and a time when faith was universal: "Dr. Johnson seemed quite wrapt up in the contemplation of the scenes which were now presented to him. He kept his hat off while he was upon any part of the ground where the cathedral had stood. . . . As we walked in the cloisters, there was a solemn echo, while he talked loudly of a proper retirement from the world" (V.62). Or contemplating, in the remains of a Highland castle, symbols of a feudal world where survival depended on moats and battlements: "the old tower must be of great antiquity. There is a drawbridge,—what has been a moat,— and an ancient court. . . . The thickness of the walls, the small slaunting windows, and a great iron door . . . all indicate the rude times in which this castle was erected" (V.119–20). Or observing, in the mementos preserved in Highland houses, relics of an age more heroic than his own: "we looked at Rorie More's horn. . . . It holds rather more than a bottle and a half. . . . We also saw his bow, which hardly any man now can bend, and his *Glaymore*, which was wielded with both hands, and is of prodigious size" (V.212).

By themselves the ruined cathedrals and decaying castles of the *Tour* would perhaps invoke only a general impression of the remote past, but between them lies the barren landscape of the Highlands, presenting "nothing but wild, moorish, hilly, and craggy appearances," where a traveler discovers his own insignificance as a man: "we had many showers, and it soon grew pretty dark. Dr. Johnson sat silent and patient. Once he said, as he looked on the black coast of Sky,—black, as being composed of rocks seen in the dusk,—'This is very solemn' " (V.257). From the time when feudal warriors fought their battles and monks prayed in ancient cloisters here, life in the Hebrides has been a precarious enterprise, and the hostile, forbidding landscape has remained the same. In such a setting, present dissolves insensibly into past, and the atmosphere of the *Tour* moves toward that of romance, which imaginatively embraces both. We are often reminded, when the travelers are moving through the Highlands, of a passage from Johnson's *Journey to the Western Islands:* "the fictions of the *Gothick* romances were not so remote from credibility as they are now thought. In the full prevalence of the feudal institution, when violence desolated the world, and every baron lived in a fortress, forests and castles were regularly succeeded by each other, and the adventurer might very suddenly pass from the gloom of woods, or the ruggedness of moors, to seats of plenty, gaiety, and magnificence."

The affinity of the *Tour* with romance finally rests on this evocation of an imaginary past, one inspired by Highland scenes but actually created in the mind of the observer. For the imaginative impulse suspends any specific comparison of present and past and demands instead the assent we give to poems and stories about older, simpler, more heroic times. Johnson's response to the landscape and society of the Hebrides is of course more com-

plicated than this—it includes, for one thing, a steady counterpoint of rational scepticism—but ultimately the relationship
between hero and milieu in the *Tour* involves an idea of spiritual
release: in the Hebrides Johnson can legitimately indulge a sort
of romantic nostalgia for a lost world of faith and heroes, and he
finds in that nostalgia an escape from his own inner conflict. If
the *Life of Johnson* gives us a hero alienated from his own society, living in a state of partial isolation from man and God, the
Tour gives us a Johnson who has moved out of the modern age
into a past that is above all remote from the actual, and whose
Highland journey finally becomes a metaphor of escape from
self.

   In the *Life of Johnson* we pass into the uncompromisingly
actual world of modern London. The scope of the *Life* is enormous, for Boswell saw in Johnson's London a microcosm of eighteenth-century England. His narrative embraces all of English
society from the drawing-room to the gutter: "he gave us an
entertaining account of *Bet Flint*, a woman of the town. . . . 'I
used to say of her, that she was generally slut and drunkard;—
occasionally whore and thief. . . . Poor Bet was taken up on the
charge of stealing a counterpane, and tried at the Old Bailey.
Chief Justice ———, who loved a wench, summed up favorably,
and she was acquitted. After which, Bet said, with a gay and
satisfied air, "Now that the counterpane is *my own*, I shall make
a petticoat of it" ' " (IV.103). This is the boisterous low-mimetic
world of Defoe and Fielding and Smollett, a noisy world of
shops, coaches, and taverns, where lord and hostler jostle each
other in the dirty streets and life is gazed at through the steady
medium of bourgeois consciousness. The distance between this
unheroic present and a nobler past is the distance between *Moll
Flanders* and the *Aeneid*.

   Yet the *Life* also gives us a hero who, in his moral and intellectual nature, is superior to such a world. Again we come to the
principle of generic tension: when Boswell compares the *Life*

to Homeric epic or invokes Plutarch as a biographical model (I.13), he is calling to mind a conception of heroic character shaped by high-mimetic convention, and from the beginning of the *Life* we see Johnson's "extraordinary powers of mind" being translated into an abstract idea of greatness, one which is described in language appropriate to the reality of an earlier age: "Johnson did not strut or stand on tip-toe; he only did not stoop. From his earliest years, his superiority was perceived and acknowledged. He was from the beginning Ἄναξ ἀνδρῶν, a king of men" (I.47). Boswell's larger portrayal of Johnson's character must of course earn our whole assent—to describe the half-blind son of a poor provincial bookseller as a "king of men" is otherwise to risk a collapse into the mock-heroic—but it is finally his invocation of an older heroic ideal that gives it moral substance. From Johnson's youth in Lichfield to the final days in London, with the crisis "fast approaching, when he must *'die like men, and fall like one of the Princes'* " (IV.398–99), we perceive his resemblance to the noble protagonists of epic and tragedy.

The tension between hero and milieu in the *Life* includes elements of both comedy and tragedy, but the comic vitality of Boswell's greatest scenes forms only a basic counterpoint to the theme of tragic isolation. For the low mimetic world of the *Life* is also the one described in Bertrand Bronson's *Johnson Agonistes*, a world caught up in a process of desperate change, where philosophies like "Hume and Voltaire and Rousseau supply momentum, and are joined by the multitude of tributaries, the freethinkers, and levellers, who all sweep giddily toward the cascade of the '90s."[8] The *Life* shows us an age where "the gallantry and military spirit of the old English nobility" has shrunk into low commercialism—" 'Why, my Lord, I'll tell you what is become of it: it has gone into the city to look for a fortune' " (II.126)— where "love of liberty" as an abstract doctrine masks a dark threat of social anarchy—" 'I believe we hardly wish that the mob should have liberty to govern us. When that was the case some time ago,

no man was at liberty not to have candles in his windows' "
(III.338)—where sceptics like Hume and atheists like Holbach
have undermined the very foundations of religious faith—in short,
where "old opinions, feelings,—ancestral customs and institutions are crumbling away, and both the spiritual and temporal
worlds are darkened by the shadow of change."[9]

The *Life* is partly the story of Johnson's heroic resistance to
these invisible forces of moral anarchy, but its larger theme concerns the cost of such resistance to mind and soul. The fierce wit
of Johnson's attacks on the philosophes and freethinkers of the
Life has a kind of desperation about it, for his impassioned orthodoxy is finally an attempt to discover certainty where there
is only doubt. When the illusion fails, there is paralysis and isolation, revealing the Johnson who, after the death of his wife,
describes himself as " 'a solitary wanderer in the wild of life,
without any direction, or fixed point of view: a gloomy gazer on
a world to which I have little relation' " (I.277). The theme of
Johnson's melancholy in the *Life* begins in its portrayal of a
world that has lost the spiritual coherence that gives meaning to
activity and certainty to belief—" 'when I survey my past life, I
discover nothing but a barren waste of time, with some . . . disturbances of mind, very near to madness, which I hope He that
made me will suffer to extenuate many faults' " (III.99)—and
where the existence of the hero turns into the inner struggle
which Boswell describes so movingly: "his mind resembled the
vast amphitheater, the Colisæum at Rome. In the centre stood his
judgement, which like a mighty gladiator, combatted those apprehensions that, like the wild beasts of the *Arena*, were all
around in cells, ready to be let out upon him. After a conflict,
he drives them back into their dens; but not killing them, they
were still assailing him" (II.106).

The affinity of the *Life* with formal tragedy lies in the story of
Johnson's personal struggle and the concept of spiritual isolation
that lies behind it, a concept large enough to embrace even the

typical image of Johnson, all "vigorous intellect and lively imagination," dominating some animated social scene. For company and talk are Johnson's constant escape from inner conflict—"the great business of his life (he said) was to escape from himself"—and even his moments of most brilliant conversation represent the efforts of a mind that has won only a temporary compromise with despair; "all the flashes of pleasure and glee in the *Life*," as David Passler has written, "are only momentary reprieves from the dark pain of existence."[10] The darker side of the hero's existence is revealed in his *Prayers and Meditations*, and in drawing on them in the course of the narrative Boswell returns again and again to the same theme—"what philosophick heroism was it in him to appear with such manly fortitude to the world when he was inwardly so distressed!"—until we perceive the pathos that surrounds even the great conversation scenes of the *Life* and the spectre of isolation that lurks behind them all. From the beginning Boswell's conception of the hero contained a potentiality for tragedy, but only in the *Life* does he emerge as a genuinely tragic figure.

The situation of the hero in Boswellian narrative is symbolically the situation of man living in an age where reason has gone to war with faith, where abstract theories of social progress have triumphed over an older wisdom of tradition and continuity, and where society has become the enemy of the free self. In conceiving of his heroes as figures associated with a past in which individualism was possible, Boswell was again anticipating an idea that would not fully emerge until the nineteenth century; for, as John Stuart Mill would argue in *On Liberty*, "in ancient history . . . and in a diminishing degree through the long transition from feudality to the present time, the individual was a power in himself; and if he had either great talents or a high social position, he was a great power. At present individuals are lost in the crowd." Yet if Paoli and Johnson represent superior natures cut off from an older community of shared belief, they are a long way from the modern antihero, groping his way around in a world of relativism and meaninglessness, for in Boswell the memory of a nobler past is still close enough to offer a kind of moral refuge and to remind the modern age of what it has lost.

This is what allows Boswell, even while he is exploring the theme of spiritual isolation, to portray Paoli and Johnson as exemplary figures, observing certain conventions of encomiastic form that go back to Plutarch. For Boswellian narrative retains the ethical emphases of classical biographical writing, which conceived of history as philosophy teaching by examples. Or even, as Dryden argued in a neoclassical essay on Plutarch, as something superior to philosophy, for "there is nothing of the tyrant in example, but it gently glides into us, is easy and pleasant in its passage, and in one word reduces into practice our speculative notions." Thus Paoli becomes a type of the stoic hero, embodying an ethical ideal otherwise to be found only in books: "it is impossible for me, speculate as I pleased, to have a little idea of human nature in him." And thus Boswell speaks of Johnson, in the *Tour to the Hebrides*, as "one whose virtues will, I hope, ever be an object of imitation," and in the *Life* offers his hero's "strong, clear, and animated enforcement of religion, morality, loyalty, and subordination" as a moral antidote to the false philosophy imported from revolutionary France.

Even here, however, we meet with the familiar principle of generic tension, for the encomiastic premise makes sense only in a moral context that permits emulation, and in Boswell this is already a thing of the past. Boswell manages to retain the ethical emphases of ancient biography only because he portrays his heroes as men who do in a sense exist in the past, operating within a structure of personal belief which is the private equivalent of the large moral unity that sustained earlier great men. Thus we have, in the *Tour to Corsica*, the Paoli who "just lives in the times of antiquity"; in the *Tour to the Hebrides*, the Johnson for whom Jacobitism and feudalism and medieval Christianity still exert something of a romantic appeal; and, preeminently, the hero of the *Life of Johnson*, whose Toryism and religious orthodoxy and monarchical principles look to a past that exists only in the imagination, and that becomes the besieged fortress of his separate faith.

Boswell's conception of the hero contains a fatal irony, for no system of personal values can replace the spiritually coherent world of the past. Paoli and Johnson are great and admirable men, but only a generous and hopeful self-delusion stands between them and the unheroic present, as when Paoli pretends that a character formed on Plutarch and Livy is wanted in the modern age, or Johnson that his lifelong contest with "Whiggery" is still a real and equal contest, something actually being decided in the world outside. For both, this private structure of belief is only an illusive affirmation of self—the refusal of a great nature to give in to the unheroic world. This is why Carlyle saw Johnson as a hero, and why the eighteenth century responded so eagerly to Paoli, the incarnation of an ancient heroic ideal. In the end the Boswellian hero is only a character in a larger drama of the self, one in which life itself becomes, in Pater's words, "the impression of the individual in his isolation, each mind keeping as a solitary prisoner its own dream of the world."

I

A PLUTARCHAN HERO
THE *TOUR TO CORSICA*

"I SAID to General Paoli," wrote Boswell in 1783, "it was wonderful how much Corsica had done for me, how far I had got in the world by having been there. I had got upon a rock in Corsica and jumped into the middle of life."[1] Boswell probably wrote the remark down because he was taken with his own mot, but it is scarcely an exaggeration. In February 1768, at the age of twenty-seven, Boswell permanently emerged from literary obscurity with the publication of his *Account of Corsica: The Journal of a Tour to That Island, and Memoirs of Pascal Paoli.* Only readers who have taken an interest in Boswell's literary career will perhaps recall how successful the book really was: immediately after its first publication *Corsica* went through two more English and several (pirated) Irish editions, was translated into French, Dutch, German, and Italian, and won Boswell an international literary reputation greater than that of either Goldsmith or Johnson.[2]

Boswell published his *Tour to the Hebrides* and *Life of Johnson*, the two works that guaranteed his permanent place in literature, in the ten years prior to his death. In the earlier years it was *Corsica* that established his literary identity: "Corsica Boswell" was, like "Dictionary Johnson," the figure with which a large contemporary public was most familiar. In a sense the response to *Corsica* marked the high point of Boswell's career as a living writer, for in that book Boswell appealed to the mind of Europe in a manner that the *Tour to the Hebrides* or the *Life of Johnson*

could never have done. But if the historical moment in which
Corsica was written accounted for much of its success, it is wrong
to infer that the book made Boswell's literary reputation because
a large European reading public, entranced by Rousseauistic
notions of primitivism and liberty, was waiting to lionize the
first young man who should write a book about a peasant rebellion. In responding to *Corsica* Boswell's readers were responding
primarily to Paoli, a figure closer to the heroic world of Plutarch
than to that of the *Contrat Social.*

For the modern reader who wishes to approach the *Tour to
Corsica* as a literary work, a brief description of the background
of events against which the book was written will suffice. The
island of Corsica, under the domination of the Republic of Genoa
since the fourteenth century, was in revolt. Over a period of
about thirty years the islanders had driven their Genoese rulers
from the interior of Corsica and forced them to take garrisoned
positions in towns along the seacoast. In 1764 the Genoese called
upon France for aid, and French troops were sent to protect the
fortified towns. Considering the formal alliance between France
and Genoa in the matter of Corsica, relations between the Corsican rebels and the French troops stationed on the island were
surprisingly polite. It was Genoa and the Genoese whom the
Corsicans hated and from whom they were determined to win
their independence after four centuries of harsh rule.

This much, or a little more, Rousseau knew when he first
praised the Corsicans for their valiant defense of liberty, and
Boswell knew when, fresh from his remarkable siege of Rousseau
at Môtiers, he set out for Corsica. There were, to be sure, certain
hardheaded citizens of the diplomatic community who shared no
romantic illusions about the island: "to Chesterfield, who reflected the view of the diplomats of Europe, the people were a
'parcel of cruel and perifidious rascals,' " and Lord Holland, even
in the face of Boswell's overwhelming success with *Corsica*, pronounced them "the vile inhabitants of one of the vilest islands

in the world, who are not less free than all the rest of their neighbours."[3] But diplomats, burdened as they are with factual reports, are denied the helpful insufficiency of information that
allows the rest of us to romanticize at will. Today the actual character of the Corsicans and the merits of their cause are perhaps
impossible to ascertain. In Boswell's time the significance of the
events on Corsica was that they were actual, and this alone had
great appeal in a political context so far dominated by theory.

Corsica as a ready-made symbol drew the attention of political
theorists whose concept of liberty, and whose notions of the
human state most conducing to liberty, needed illustration; "a
generation profoundly stirred by theories of the progressive corruption of governments and the glories of the state of nature," as
F. A. Pottle puts it, "found that it no longer had to look to the
remote past or the world of ideas for its example of the good
state, or at least of a state which held promise of becoming
good."[4] In Frederick of Prussia's *Anti-Machiavel*, therefore, contemporary readers came across a reference to Corsica "in which
this 'little handful of brave men' were cited to prove how much
courage and natural virtue the love of liberty bestowed upon
men"[5] and in a famous passage of the *Contrat Social* (1762) reflected on Rousseau's remark that "in the midst of almost hope-
less governmental corruption, there was one country still capable
of legislation, and that he had a presentiment that the little island
of Corsica would one day astonish Europe."[6]

Rousseau's remark led in turn to the complicated business of
Corsica's constitution. The affair is rather too involved to go into
here, but the essential facts are simple enough: as a result of the
passage in the *Contrat Social*, Rousseau was invited, or thought
he was invited, by the rebel leaders of Corsica to compose a constitution on which the government of the island was to be founded
after it had won its independence. He actually began the project.
As the very idea of a constitution written *en philosophe* indicates,
what Rousseau and his fellow theorists saw in Corsica was a

utopian potentiality. Though it was perhaps a general scarcity
of information which led Rousseau to comment on Corsica's
promise as an independent state, it was clear to some Corsicans
that this promise could best be fulfilled if the state engaged a
Rousseau to write it into being. The emphasis is not on Corsica
itself but on process, on becoming; the island is only the local
habitation of a theory.

When he made his tour to Corsica, Boswell was in his period
of greatest allegiance to Rousseau's social and political theories.
But what is too little noted is that neither Rousseau nor Boswell
knew very much about Corsica and that what both of them saw
in Corsica was a grand potentiality for idealization. We have
Boswell's response in *Corsica;* about Rousseau's we can be less
sure, for the constitution of Corsica was never finished (and,
since Corsica lost its war of independence, it could never have
been put into effect). What we do have of Rousseau's constitution, however, forms an important commentary on Boswell's
portrait of the islanders. Corsica as a free state, according to
Rousseau's prescription, was to form a society simple, virtuous,
peaceful, and independent: "the object was to turn the Corsicans
into a nation of farmers, and very literally to beat swords into
plough-shares. The island was to be self-supporting and independent of commerce with its neighbours. 'Le seul moyen,'
wrote Rousseau, 'de maintenir un État dans l'indépendance des
autres est l'agriculture.' For this reason his entire plan is a 'sys-
tème rustique.' "[7]

The picture is utopian, and behind it, in nearly undisguised
form, is the myth of the Golden Age dressed up as modern political theory. I have little doubt that it was this utopian potentiality, and Corsica's more practical potentiality for complete
self-sufficiency ("un État dans l'indépendance des autres"), that
initially attracted Boswell to Corsica, though he was to develop
the implications of both in a manner that Rousseau would have
found uncongenial. In any event Boswell arrived in Corsica in a

frame of mind that entirely accounts for the character of the
book he later wrote: "the *Account* and the *Journal and Memoirs*," William Siebenschuh explains, "form a single and continuous piece of propaganda and were intended to function together
to influence public opinion in Britain."[8] As important, Boswell
shared with Rousseau at this point a tendency to romanticize the
Corsicans themselves, not their leader.

When Boswell arrived in Corsica, however, he was not long in
hearing from the islanders themselves about the character of
Pascal Paoli. From the time Boswell meets Paoli, or, more properly, from the time he first divines Paoli's real role on Corsica,
his tendency to idealize takes a new direction entirely. The result, to those of us who are able to gaze back at *Corsica* through
the *Tour to the Hebrides* and the *Life of Johnson*, will seem natural, even inevitable: after Boswell's meeting with Paoli, everything is subordinated to the figure of the hero. The tendency that
Boswell shared with Rousseau, to celebrate the Corsicans for
their bravery in defense of liberty, is utterly transformed, and
Boswell ends by idealizing the Corsicans themselves not to illus-
trate any social or political theory but to provide his hero with a
proper moral setting.

Boswell's gravitation toward the figure of Paoli as hero accounts in part for what the modern reader will perceive as a
small paradox: given the historical moment and the influence of
Rousseau's theories on Boswell, *Corsica* might be described as a
reactionary book. The ancient ideal of the Philosopher King
and implicit suggestions of a conscious feudalism animate Boswell's portrait of Paoli and the Corsicans much more than the
current of democratic or egalitarian ideas that we see today as
having led to the American and French revolutions. In this, as
much as in his simpler tendency to find and idealize a hero, Boswell was showing an attitude that was to remain consistent
throughout his literary career. Intellectual historians tell us that
there is a large and inevitable conservative component in any set

of radical ideas, and the contemporary success of Boswell's *Corsica* illustrates the point perfectly. In the *Tour to the Hebrides* and the *Life of Johnson* one inevitably notes the relation of Boswell's concept of the hero to a conservative ideal, but it can only surprise us to find that same ideal at work in the *Tour to Corsica*, a book that purports to be about liberty and political rebellion.

At the same time, one cannot really disagree with the usual contention that the intellectual climate of the mid-eighteenth century was such that a book about any rebellion like the one in Corsica was likely to be warmly received. But, properly speaking, it was Boswell's *Account of Corsica*, the quasi-scholarly study of Corsican history and politics which preceded his personal journal, that satisfied this topical interest. Even with the climate of opinion as it was, I would guess that the *Tour to Corsica*, revolving around the portrait of Paoli, was accepted more for its literary than for its topical appeal. This at any rate is what Johnson had in mind when he uttered what is perhaps the most famous criticism of *Corsica:* "your History was copied from books; your Journal rose out of your own experience and observation. You express images which operated strongly upon yourself, and you have impressed them with great force upon your readers. I know not whether I could name any narrative by which curiosity is better excited or better gratified."

Johnson was correct. It is Boswell's *Tour* that survives, and properly so, for it belongs to literature. The image that operated most strongly on Boswell's imagination, as Johnson indirectly acknowledges, was the image of the hero. The book whose title we today shorten to *Corsica* is of course the second part of Boswell's account of the island, the first-person narrative that Johnson calls his journal. This short work, so successful in its own time, is at once a fine job of historical reporting and a small literary classic, and it does much to define the nature of Boswell's later achievement. For when Boswell set out for Corsica with an unconscious intention to idealize the Corsican people and their

fight for liberty, he participated in the attitude of such philosophes as Rousseau and, more generally, in that main current of
"progressive" ideas we now associate with the Enlightenment.
But as soon as that tendency to idealize is shaped by the dominant
figure of the hero, we have the first expression of an impulse that
was to remain consistent with Boswell through his entire literary
career.

TWO

In literature, especially high-mimetic literature, we are accustomed to the notion of an idealized social or political order which
forms a background to the actions of the hero. Reference to this
order may be implicit, as with the *comitatus* relationship in
Beowulf, or explicit, as with the fellowship of the Round Table
in *Sir Gawain* or the *Morte Darthur,* but it is there, the indis-
pensable context for our understanding of the hero's character.
In the *Tour to Corsica* we have an analogue of this familiar motif
in Boswell's portrait of the islanders. The reader of the *Tour* is
intended to view Paoli as a character in history and not in epic or
tragedy, but just as his resemblance to the high-mimetic hero is
calculated, so is the support it gains from Boswell's description
of Corsican society.

In idealizing Corsican society, Boswell is locating Paoli as hero
within an order that makes his heroism comprehensible and consistent. The device is conventional, and its importance perhaps
becomes clear when we consider that the hero *outside* such an
order is a traditional type of madman—the psychotic Napoleon
sitting in the psychiatrist's waiting room, for example. Without
the social context Boswell supplies, Paoli would appear in the
Tour to Corsica as a figure not heroic but ludicrous, and the solemnity with which Boswell treats certain aspects of his character—his claims to second sight, his moments of spontaneous

oratory—would become, if anything, hugely comic. What prevents this from happening is the presence, around Paoli, of people who believe in him as a hero and whose moral qualities underscore his own high moral character.

The character of the Corsican people as Boswell draws it, however, places them in a simpler world than we associate with either epic or tragedy and arises not least from their situation as inhabitants of an island. Islands are not necessarily literary symbols, though (like roses) they are perhaps as often as they are not; what makes an island symbolic is the stress the narrator lays on its remoteness from the known world, from the familiar, the everyday, and quite often the corrupt. Boswell's portrait of the Corsican people lays great moral emphasis on the remoteness of Corsica from Europe, or more precisely from European consciousness. (Similarly, in the *Account of Corsica*, which precedes the *Tour*, Boswell goes to some lengths to identify Corsica's long line of political oppressors with the corrupt world from which Corsica is separated by the sea, the world of secret treaties, expedient alliances, broken promises, power politics, and Machiavellian statecraft generally.) This is why the Genoese, as the villains of the *Tour*, are portrayed as the local representatives, merely, of an advanced but decayed civilization, as intruders in a simple rural world.

The separation of Corsica from the rest of Europe is thus a moral as well as a geographical fact. In discovering this symbolic significance in the island situation of the Corsicans, and in the difference between the national characters of the Genoese and the Corsicans, Boswell is in one sense aligning Corsica with the utopian islands of western literature, with Plato's Atlantis, More's Utopia, Bacon's New Atlantis. Corsica simply as an island would not necessarily possess this utopian significance, but Boswell in the *Tour* is describing Corsica during its battle for independence and (more important) Corsica under Paoli. For Boswell these are crucial factors, enabling him to present Corsican society as a

potentially ideal order struggling to assert itself against corrupt
and crushing opposition. The effect of this is to place Boswell,
as the only European who has come to Corsica and grasped the
moral significance of what is happening there, in the position of
a Raphael Hythloday. This is the meaning of Paoli's plea that
Boswell tell his story to the British court: "tell them what you
have seen here. They will be curious to ask you. A man come
from Corsica will be like a man come from the Antipodes" (186).

As Boswell makes clear from the beginning, he has been drawn
not to a place but to a drama of events, an ideal actually working
itself out in the state of nature: "Corsica occurred to me as a
place which nobody else had seen, and where I should find what
was to be seen nowhere else, a people actually fighting for liberty and forming themselves from a poor, inconsiderable, op-
pressed nation into a flourishing and independent state" (156).
At the beginning of the *Tour* Boswell offers himself as a typical
representative of European culture, unsure about what he is
going to find on Corsica but prepared to meet with a civilization
that, insofar as it is different from his own, will be primitive and
barbaric. His first picture of Corsican life is based on a conversation with a British naval officer who has visited several ports on
the island and who solemnly assures Boswell that he is risking his
life "in going among these barbarians," for his own surgeon's
mate had once gone ashore on Corsica "to take the diversion of
shooting and every moment was alarmed by some of the natives
who started from the bushes with loaded guns and, if he had not
been protected by Corsican guides, would have certainly blown
out his brains" (157). The British officer's account belongs to
the genre of imaginary adventures in which white men sail beside
savage coasts, pursued by painted barbarians who run along the
shoreline howling and brandishing spears.

The officer's encapsulated portrait of the Corsicans as savage
barbarians is the exact reverse of the romantic primitivism that
Boswell eventually appeals to in idealizing Corsican society. But
for now it is offered as typical of the average European's attitude

toward Corsica, one which will be displaced to great effect by a view of the Corsicans not as savages but as people virtuously close to simple nature. This second view begins to emerge with Boswell's first sight of some actual Corsican natives, who emerge suddenly from the idyllic landscape: "the prospect of the mountains covered with vines and olives was extremely agreeable, and the odour of the myrtle and other aromatic shrubs and flowers that grew all around me was very refreshing. As I walked along, I often saw Corsican peasants come suddenly out from the covert; and as they were all armed, I saw how the frightened imagination of the surgeon's mate had raised up so many assassins" (160). As dusk gathers, and Boswell continues on his way, he thinks of some lines from Ariosto: "e pur per selva oscure e calli obliqui / Insieme van senza sospetto aversi." The error of the British officer, in other words, and of his surgeon's mate, has been one not of fact but of imaginative response: *hony soyt qui mal y pense.*

As Boswell begins to lose his European prejudice about Corsica, he responds with increasing admiration to the social character formed by the rude simplicity of life on the island. On his passage to Corsica by boat, he earlier glimpsed this character in his conversation with some Corsican natives—"they told me that in their country I should be treated with the greatest hospitality, but if I attempted to debauch any of their women I might expect instant death" (159)—but with Boswell's arrival on the island the picture of a people formed by nature is filled in, and the young traveler from Britain beholds a nation of simple, hardy, virtuous citizens with a stern sense of honor and a profound potentiality for feeling shame. Boswell's description of the hangman of Corsica epitomizes the theme of honor and shame: "being held in the utmost detestation, he durst not live like another inhabitant of the island. He was obliged to take refuge in the Castle, and there he was kept in a little corner turret . . . for nobody would have any intercourse with him, but all turned their backs upon him" (167).

This hangman is a Sicilian recruited by Paoli for the task, for no Corsican could be brought to agree to execute his country-men, "not the greatest criminals, who might have had their lives upon that condition" (168). From Boswell's description of the hangman's situation, there is perhaps little in this to surprise us: the life of the state executioner in Corsica seems only barely preferable to a quick death as a convicted criminal. But that, of course, is not the point, nor is it strictly the uprightness of Cor-sican criminals. In a state where the principles of personal honor and shame transcend those embodied in laws or religion, there is a potentiality for loyalty and honorable action that does not ex-ist in more advanced, and therefore more cynical, nations. It is this aspect of the Corsican character that the hangman incident dramatizes: if the behavior of a society's worst element is thus controlled by an overwhelming sense of possible shame, what capacity for the same feelings will be shown by its best, even its ordinary, citizens?

Among Corsica's ordinary citizens, in fact, the principle of personal honor embraces a patriotism based on the related notion of national honor. Honor and patriotism among the Corsicans are part of an extralegal morality that leads to attitudes not found in more "civilized" states and from which Corsica's utopian promise in the deepest sense derives. The interplay of personal honor and loyalty to Corsica as a state appears in Paoli's account of his conversation with the nephew of a condemned Corsican criminal. The nephew's proposal is that his uncle be banished from Corsica, and he offers the guarantee of his family that the uncle will never return to the island. Paoli counters with a direct appeal to the young man's sense of national honor: " 'such is my confidence in you, that if you will say that giving your uncle a pardon would be just, useful, or honourable for Corsica, I promise you it will be granted.' He turned about and burst into tears, and left me, saying, 'I would not have the honour of our country sold for a thousand zechins.' And his uncle suffered" (182).

The *Tour to Corsica* powerfully invokes, in such scenes, an

attitude toward undeveloped human societies which the eighteenth century was finding increasingly persuasive and which
will support Boswell's eventual appeal to the older myth of the
Golden Age. Boswell himself, making sure that no one will miss
the philosophical point, includes in the *Tour* an excerpt that nice-
ly exemplifies the new primitivism, taken from a work surprisingly entitled *A Comparative View of the State and Faculties of
Man with Those of the Animal World*, by a Doctor Gregory:
" 'there is a certain period in the progress of society in which
mankind appear to the greatest advantage. In this period, they
have the bodily powers and all the animal functions remaining
in full vigour. They are bold, active, steady, ardent in the love
of liberty and their native country. Their manners are simple,
their social affections warm, and though they are greatly influenced by the ties of blood, yet they are generous and hospitable to strangers. Religion is universally regarded among them,
though disguised by a variety of superstitions' " (180).

From this, romantic primitivism dressed up as science, Boswell
develops his complicated appeal to the myth of the Golden Age.
Not *the* myth, one should say, for despite the eighteenth century's
conversance with classical tradition, no single Golden Age myth
had universal currency, and even if there had been one, Boswell's
portrait of Corsican society contains elements that surely would
not have been compatible with it. Yet Boswell moves inescapably
toward that accumulation of mythic material we usually charac-
terize as proto-pastoral, and his point of departure is the golden
pastoral world we encounter in the *Georgics* or in certain poems
by Horace. This is not, properly speaking, the golden age of
mythic prehistory but a state in which existence is simple, peaceful, and self-sufficient, mostly because of its close harmony with
nature, and which is an island in a busy, corrupt and mercenary
world. It is the world we expect to come upon in classical literature when we discover a hardy, healthy people thriving on a bare
sufficiency of acorns and water. This, as we have seen, is the

world Boswell finds himself in when he temporarily leaves off
riding horseback and joins his Corsican guides on foot: "when
we grew hungry, we threw stones among the thick branches of
the chestnut trees which overshadowed us, and in that manner
we brought down a shower of chestnuts with which we filled our
pockets, and went on eating them with great relish; and when
this made us thirsty, we lay down by the side of the first brook,
put our mouths to the stream and drank sufficiently. It was just
being for a while one of the 'prisca gens mortalium' who ran
about in the woods eating acorns and drinking water" (168–69).

The phrase that Boswell includes in his own stream of impressions is from Horace's second Epode, and readers of Horace will
recall that this is the poem in which an idyllic invocation of the
golden pastoral world is abruptly undercut by an ending which
sets all that has gone before in a severely ironic context: "haec ubi
locutus faenerator Alfius . . ." The reminder of the outside world
which Horace introduces in the figure of Alfius the usurer is not
out of place in the *Tour to Corsica*, for we are not to take Boswell's identification of the Corsicans with the "prisca gens mortalium" simply and by itself, but always to recognize that he is
describing a threatened state of virtuous simplicity, that his Corsica, like Horace's imaginary rural farm, exists only precariously
in a world governed by corrupt men and mercenary motives.
The Rome of Horace's Alfius is, in the *Tour*, a Europe which
wishes to encroach on the ideal society existing in the interior of
Corsica.

From this pastoral myth, classical in origin and association,
Boswell moves to a closely related ideal, that of Christian religious retirement. The path Boswell takes through the island
moves from convent to convent (there are few inns on Corsica)
and repeatedly provides an opportunity to evoke the picture of
honest, pious, hospitable monks, morally sustained in their holy
life by the larger simplicity of the Corsican society that exists
beyond the convent walls. Thus the worthy Rector of Cuttoli,

to choose a typical figure, is "directly such a venerable hermit as we read of in the old romances," and thus life in the convent at Corte represents a peaceful and otherworldly idyll:

> These fathers have a good vineyard and an excellent garden. They have between thirty and forty beehives in long wooden cases or trunks of trees, with a covering of the bark of the cork tree. When they want honey they burn a little juniper-wood, the smoke of which makes the bees retire. They then take an iron instrument with a sharp-edged crook at one end of it and bring out the greatest part of the honeycomb, leaving only a little for the bees, who work the case full again. By taking the honey in this way they never kill a bee. They seemed much at their ease, living in peace and plenty. I often joked with them on the text which is applied to their order: "Nihil habentes et omnia possidentes." (165)

Boswell is charmed by precisely those elements that this scene of religious retirement shares with the classical world of golden pastoral, the peacefulness and simplicity of life in the convent at Corte, its self-sufficiency and harmony with nature. This is another appeal to primitivism, and the simple piety of the monks is the only specifically religious coloring that Boswell adds to the picture. Those sterner motives that we usually associate with the impulse to leave the world and enter a monastery—a desire for self-abnegation and sacrifice, a conscious acceptance of a rigorous life devoted to self-examination and prayer—are excluded. Boswell's convent at Corte is close to the world of the *Ancrene Riwle* and far from the hair shirts and self-flagellation that is the other side of our idea of monastery life.

Yet the holy life of the fathers at Corte exists as precariously as does the rest of Paoli's tiny nation, and a force which is not strictly compatible with this idyll of simplicity and peace has arisen to defend it. No Golden Age myth, so far as I am aware, allows for the presence of an armed and warlike populace, for peace among men is one of the ideal effects of simple virtue and harmony with nature. Yet we recognize the Golden Age as an informing element in the background of romance and realize that some sort of reconciliation of apparent opposites has taken place when we encounter jarring violence in the pastoral landscapes of Ariosto or *The Faerie Queene*. There is no overt violence in the *Tour to Corsica*, but the possibilities of a symbolic disjunction are there, and it is a tribute to Boswell's modulation from the purely pastoral to the militaristic that we feel both to be parts of a consistent whole.

Boswell's portrait of the Corsicans as warriors has no one model, though its outline follows the idea of military simplicity and hardihood that we have agreed to call Spartan. Through it Boswell is able to remind us constantly that Corsica is a beleaguered state whose battle for independence is a moral as well as a military struggle, showing the forces of a corrupt outside world arrayed against the simple citizens of a political order that is uncorrupt and close to nature. Corsica is defended by citizen patriots whose ardor is closely related to her simplicity as a polity, and at times Boswell seems to be moving through scenes that recall the military and civil virtues of earliest Rome. Because Corsica is in a state of siege, foreigners are viewed with suspicion, and it is deemed advisable at one point that Boswell get a passport to carry with him into the interior: "after supper, therefore, the Prior walked with me to Corte to the house of the Great Chancellor, who ordered the passport to be made out immediately. . . . When the passport was finished and ready to have the seal put on it, I was much pleased with a beautiful, simple incident. The Chancellor desired a little boy who was playing in the room by us to run to his mother and bring the great seal of the kingdom. I thought myself sitting in the house of a Cincinnatus" (168).

The Corsicans as warriors belong, really, to the half-mythic world of Cincinnatus. The islanders are, as soldiers, brave, self-disciplined, inured to hardship, and have a sense of personal honor that finds its social counterpart in a total and all-inclusive patriotism. This portrait takes on a pastoral coloring, and the strictly military virtues of the Corsicans remind us more than anything else of the last six books of the *Aeneid*, of the world of Turnus and his compatriots, of simple bravery and battle carried out against a pastoral setting. Yet there are also elements which are not strictly associated with any classical context, and more than one passage in the *Tour* is likelier to recall the image of the American frontiersman, in his ideal and mythic state, than of Virgil.

De Toqueville, perhaps, or those who have called the frontier the American version of pastoral, would immediately recognize the symbolic background in Boswell's description of the "stately, spirited race of people" he finds at Bastelica: "they just came in, making an easy bow, placed themselves round the room where I was sitting, rested themselves on their muskets, and immediately entered into conversation with me" (169); or of this scene of Corsicans at their leisure: "the chief satisfaction of these islanders, when not engaged in war or in hunting, seemed to be that of lying at their ease in the open air, recounting tales of the bravery of their countrymen, and singing songs in honour of the Corsicans and against the Genoese. Even in the night they will continue this pastime in the open air, unless rain forces them to retire into their houses" (184–85). When *Corsica* was written, the American frontier had yet to be mythologized, but Boswell's portrait of the Corsican soldiers anticipates the mythic impulse that would eventually make legends not only of the hardy frontiersmen of American folklore but of the ragged band of citizen soldiers who began a revolution at Concord and Lexington. The figures of the American myth arose from the eighteenth-century fable of man's freedom and dignity in the state of nature, and Boswell's Corsicans belong to their family.

Corsica in its state of siege, however, is not the American frontier, for the rough simplicity of these scenes coexists with an idea of polite civilization that even now is implicitly present in the rude interior of the island, awaiting only the blessing of political

independence to emerge. Rousseau's vision of the state into which
Corsica might develop after independence depended heavily on
an idea of agrarian anonymity: "la nation ne sera point illustre,
mais elle sera heureuse. On ne parlera pas d'elle; elle aura peu de
consideration au dehors; mais elle aura l'abondance, la paix et la
liberté dans son sein."[9] For Rousseau, one suspects, Corsica in its
present primitive state already represented something of a philosophical ideal, and he would only have been annoyed at any suggestion of change after independence. But Boswell was less
convinced than Rousseau that any advance in civilization involves
an inevitable and proportionate advance toward decadence. Politesse is for Boswell a social ideal with considerable appeal, and
he envisions for the Corsicans a social development that will grow
naturally from their present simplicity of life.

Corsica after independence will become a nation increasingly
self-sufficient in its economy and increasingly conversant, on a
cultural level, with more civilized states but preserving an integrity that will keep it aloof from the rapacity, duplicity, and
propensity for diplomatic intrigue that characterizes Europe.
Corsica as a free island nation need stand no danger of being
swallowed up by the corrupt world represented by her Genoese
oppressors. Even now one comes across certain scenes which
promise that Corsica will someday achieve a civilization as polished as any in Europe but without degeneration into European
luxury and decadence: "at dinner we had no less than twelve
well-dressed dishes, served on Dresden china, with a dessert, different sorts of wine, and a liqueur, all the produce of Corsica.
Signor Barbaggi was frequently repeating to me that the Corsicans inhabited a rude, uncultivated country and that they lived
like Spartans. I begged leave to ask him in what country he could
show me greater luxury than I had seen in his house" (164).

Politesse out of rugged simplicity: we glimpse the same theme
in Boswell's visit to another Corsican household, where the music
of any polite European drawing room uneasily coexists with a

more boisterous native tradition: "after they had shown me their taste in fine improved music, they gave me some original Corsican airs, and . . . a Corsican dance. It was truly savage. They thumped with their heels, sprung upon their toes, brandished their arms, wheeled and leaped with the most violent gesticulations. It gave me the idea of an admirable war-dance" (202). The ideal of polite civilization in Corsica, however, is most significantly represented in the coastal towns garrisoned by the French. One would expect, as Boswell at first expects, the Corsicans to despise the French as hirelings of the hated Genoese. But in the period Boswell is describing, a pause in Corsica's war with Genoa, relations between the Corsicans and the French are unexpectedly cordial.

This pause in Corsica's war of independence determines the mood of the *Tour*, for it lends Boswell's portrait of the Corsican people a static quality, an opportunity for leisurely discovery that lies beyond the reach of any narrative that must describe a people caught up in the violent upheaval of war. The Genoese, having deserted the island during this time of uneasy truce, never enter into the narrative directly; we do not see the oppressors but feel their presence as the Corsicans must, as a remote and menacing force whose one purpose is to swallow up the ancient society existing in the interior of the island. And the French, whose military presence serves as a constant reminder that Corsica's liberty is yet to be won, seem on the human and cultural level almost sympathetic to Corsica and her cause.

As a symbol of polite civilization the French garrison represents the politesse of European culture preserved from luxurious excess by the rigors of a military situation: a Frenchman on Corsica, though he bring with him all the easy cosmopolitanism of Paris, is on Corsica still. At the end of his tour Boswell decides to depart for the mainland from Bastia. He finds the town an island within an island, whose ruler is the Count de Marbeuf, "a worthy, open-hearted Frenchman" whose agreeable personality derives, Boswell suggests, both from his being French and a long-time army officer: "such a character is gay without levity and judicious without severity. Such a character was the Count de Marbeuf, of an ancient family in Brittany." And here, in Marbeuf's tiny dominion, exists that world of elegance and grace without which Corsican society, for all its rugged virtues, is incomplete: "next morning I waited on M. de Marbeuf.... He gave me a most polite reception. The brilliancy of his levée pleased me; it was a scene so different from those which I had been for some time accustomed to see. It was like passing at once from a rude and early age to a polished modern age, from the mountains of Corsica to the banks of the Seine" (209).

This sudden transition from the wild interior of Corsica to the polish and ease of life in the French garrison allows us finally to view the two modes of existence in sympathetic contrast. And to see the beginning of a process at work, for the retreat of the Genoese from the island, and their replacement by the French, has introduced a formative influence on Corsican society: "perhaps indeed the residence of the French in Corsica has, upon the whole, been an advantage to the patriots. There have been markets twice a week at the frontiers of each garrison town, where the Corsican peasants have sold all sorts of provisions and brought in a good many French crowns which have been melted down into Corsican money" (212). Not only has the lull in combat given the islanders time to look about them, it has given them a model to contemplate and a period of temporary peace during which they can begin to live the kind of life that will be theirs as a free society: "a cessation of arms for a few years has been a breathing time to the nation to prepare itself for one great effort, which will probably end in the total expulsion of the Genoese. A little leisure has been given for attending to civil improvements, towards which the example of the French has in no small degree contributed" (212–13).

Boswell on his arrival in Corsica was the most typical of eighteenth-century travelers, the young man of good birth whose tour of Europe was regarded as the end of his formal education. Boswell's stay in Corsica has been an interlude—an important one, one in which he has gained a new perception of history and heroism and political morality, but an interlude just the same. The story that began with the anxious imaginings of a British surgeon's mate thus closes on a similar note. Paoli has sent, as Boswell's guide to Bastia, a Corsican named Ambrosio, "a strange, iron-coloured, fearless creature. He had been much in war; careless of wounds, he was coolly intent on destroying the enemy. . . . I was sure I needed be under no apprehensions; but I don't know how, I desired Ambrosio to march before me that I might see him" (202–3). In Boswell's apprehension begins the restoration of distance that allows us to see his visit to Corsica as a romantic journey into a forgotten age and to understand his portrayal of the Corsican people as an excursion into something very close to myth.

THREE

Boswell's idealizing portrayal of the Corsican people is finally, however, a subordinate motif, for the *Tour* is really a book about Pascal Paoli, a man unknown, before Boswell introduced him, to the generality of educated Europeans but afterward acclaimed by them as a hero stepped out of antique times. Boswell's portrait of the Corsicans, we have seen, is an analogue of the idealized social order behind the hero of epic or romance, providing the dramatic context that makes the specific qualities of his heroism comprehensible. Yet if the picture of Corsican society offered in the *Tour* represents an ideal order that derives its utopian promise from the vigor and primitive simplicity of Corsican life, it is Paoli who sustains both that order and its promise. For the Corsicans as the citizenry of an unrealized commonwealth are Paoli's creation. Paoli alone has been able to bring out his people's best qualities and to suppress their worst, and he has become the symbol of their feeling for Corsica as a whole, if only because the whole would not exist without him.

In one sense, therefore, the *Tour to Corsica* appears to be dealing with the familiar theme of the great man in history, with the notion of the superior individual who, in a given historical moment, assumes power over people and the direction of events. We seem to be closest to this idea when we observe that Corsican society as we see it in the *Tour* exists only because Paoli, through sheer force of personality and moral character, has managed to bring order out of anarchy: only since he has become their ruler has the Corsican sense of personal honor been transformed into patriotism, their tendency to violence into bravery in war, and their state of existence, based on a bare agricultural subsistence, into a pastoral state holding forth the promise of becoming more. Corsica as an ideal society exists largely in Paoli's vision, and his islanders are willing to leave the matter of vision up to him, in effect to accept it at one remove, through their loyalty to their leader.

Yet Paoli does not represent what Sidney Hook has called the event-making man, the hero in history, for the nature of his heroism takes us in quite a different direction, away from the world of practical affairs and toward the world of the imagination. This involves the notion, mentioned earlier, of the past as imaginative refuge: throughout the *Tour* we see Paoli not merely as a mystic or visionary, but specifically as a heroic figure whose dream of the past is a response to his own unheroic age. The spiritual allegiance of the Corsicans to their leader is thus a participation in an illusion so compelling that for the time it has replaced reality. This is why we are aware of an idealized or even mythic quality in Boswell's portrayal of the Corsican people, for his narrative ultimately pictures a state of unreality, a state in which both the hero and his society, existing with a magic circle of illusion, live apart from the modern age.

Paoli is first felt in the *Tour* as an ideal presence. Though Boswell has arrived full of admiration for the Corsicans' struggle for liberty, he has had no intimation that behind their bravery and resolution stands the single dominant personality of a leader. But as Boswell, in his first travels through the island, discovers that every Corsican identifies the battle for independence with Paoli's aspirations for his people, he inescapably begins to perceive Paoli's role as an inspirational figure in Corsican history. This first impression is continuously reinforced, until, as Boswell tells us, he himself is almost ready to approach Paoli as someone more god-like than human: "when I at last came within sight of Sollacaro, where Paoli was, I could not help being under considerable anxiety. My ideas of him had been greatly heightened by the conversations I had held with all sorts of people in the island, they having represented him to me as something above humanity" (170).

The representations of the Corsicans, as we discover when Paoli enters the story, contain a largely imaginative truth. Paoli as a leader brings to life an idea of stoic heroism—a self-discipline taking the form of stern self-denial, a quality of true greatness which communicates itself in his manner—that takes us out of the decayed world of the mid-eighteenth century and into the times of antiquity. To encounter Paoli as a man is almost inescapably to be moved to considerations of past and present. In ancient times, Boswell tells us at one point, when noblemen were like princes in their power, they were open and affable: "some of our modern nobility are so anxious to preserve an appearance of dignity which they are sensible cannot bear an examination that they are afraid to let you come near them. Paoli is not so. Those about him come into his apartment at all hours, wake him, help him on with his clothes, are perfectly free from restraint; yet they know their distance and, awed by his real greatness, never lose their respect for him" (196).

Such scenes appeal to something like the Renaissance fable of

an aristocracy of virtue, that social myth which placed the beginnings of hereditary nobility in personal superiority; and, by
extension, to the theme of decay which is the usual accompani-
ment to the myth of the Golden Age. By so much as Paoli differs
from the decayed nobility of contemporary Europe does Corsica
differ morally from the world outside, for Paoli's distance from
the people he rules is one solely of personal authority. In the
eighteenth century, with aristocracy at the beginning of its great
modern decline but still retaining a good deal of ideological pres-
tige, the idea had a special appeal. Boswell pictures his hero as a
natural aristocrat in a natural setting, offering his audience an
implicit comparison with their own modern aristocracy, whose
place owes almost nothing to moral character and everything to
riches, inherited political influence, and, above all, the accident
of fate that made them noblemen rather than hostlers.

Paoli's manner returns Boswell again and again to the theme of
stoic heroism, for in it, the quality of "real greatness" discovered
in a man who walks the earth, lies Paoli's affinity with the heroes
of ancient myth and history: "I observed that although he had
often a placid smile upon his countenance, he hardly ever laughed.
Whether loud laughter in general society be a sign of weakness
or rusticity I cannot say; but I have remarked that real great men,
and men of finished behaviour, seldom fall into it" (176). The
idea is familiar enough to qualify as an eighteenth-century commonplace—Lord Chesterfield's *Letters* are always advising his son
that well-bred men smile but do not laugh—but only as a matter
of decorum, a social counterfeit of which Paoli's instinctive dignity is the original. Yet Paoli's greatness is far from being a matter
wholly of instinct, for Boswell's conception of the hero demands
a moral character shaped consciously, not a happy accident of
human nature. The stoic strain in Paoli's personality has been
carefully cultivated: "he observed that the Epicurean philosophy
had produced but one exalted character, whereas Stoicism had
been the seminary of great men. What he now said put me in
mind of these noble lines of Lucan:

> ... Hi mores, haec duri inmota Catonis
> Secta fuit, servare modum finemque tenere,
> Naturamque sequi patriaque inpendere vitam,
> Nec sibi toti genitum se credere mundo." (178)

"He bids your breasts with ancient ardour rise," as Pope said in his prologue to Addison's *Cato*, "And calls forth Roman drops from British eyes": in translating Paoli's preference for Stoic philosophy immediately into Lucan's vision of heroic patriotism, Boswell is appealing less to history than to stoicism as a conscious ideal, reminding us that a man who has become great through an act of moral effort is superior to one whom the gods have simply appointed as fit to lead.

Boswell's emphasis on the role of mind and will in Paoli's greatness moves us in another direction, toward the ideal of the Philosopher King. Like the Guardians of Plato's *Republic*, Paoli has been educated from birth for the leadership of his people, and his personal notions of leadership are derived entirely from philosophy and history. With a memory "like that of Themistocles," Paoli has "the best part of the classics by heart," and he moves in an imaginative world where past and present are imperceptibly merged. "I have heard him give," says Boswell, "what the French call *un catalogue raisonné* of the most distinguished men in antiquity. His characters of them were concise, nervous, and just. I regret that the fire with which he spoke upon such occasions so dazzled me that I could not recollect his sayings so as to write them down when I retired from his presence. He just lives in the times of antiquity. He said to me, 'A young man who would form his mind to glory must not read modern memoirs, but Plutarch and Titus Livius'" (190–91). Boswell clearly is dazzled less by the conciseness, nervousness, and justness of the portraits in Paoli's catalogue raisonné (what might be called their rhetorical qualities) than by the amount of imaginative and moral energy that Paoli has put into them: "he just lives in the times of antiquity."

As with Boswell's appeal to myth in his portrait of the Corsicans, the idea of Paoli as an actual hero of antiquity uses time as a metaphor of moral integrity. The *Tour* is able to present us with the vision of a people living in a Golden Age, led by a Plutarchan hero, existing precariously in the midst of a degenerate modern world, precisely because Boswell has found a way to represent convincingly the idea of moral distance in temporal terms. And the metaphor does convince, as we see in the sentence with which the *Tour* ends, Pitt's famous pronouncement on its hero: " 'it may be said of Paoli, as the Cardinal de Retz said of the great Montrose, "he is one of those men who are no longer to be found but in the *Lives* of Plutarch" ' " (216). Echoes of Pitt's reaction to Paoli are to be found throughout the record of contemporary response to the *Tour*, the response of a public whose only acquaintance with Paoli was through Boswell.[10]

Boswell's usual means of associating Paoli with the world of the ancient heroes is the allusive. Allusion in the *Tour* is a straightforward affair, occurring most often when some aspect of Paoli's character brings to mind a parallel in myth, epic, or history. Outside Paoli's chamber, for instance, sleep five or six faithful Corsican dogs: "they are extremely sagacious, and know all his friends and attendants. Were any person to approach the General during the night, they would instantly tear him in pieces. Having dogs for his attendants is another circumstance about Paoli similar to the heroes of antiquity" (197). Boswell then goes on to note parallels with Homer's descriptions of Telemachus and the family of Patroclus; to take such a passage out of context perhaps emphasizes in a way unfair to Boswell the artlessness of his mode of allusion. Yet the descriptive simplicity of the *Tour* is part of its strategy, and such allusions invariably work to deepen our sense of Paoli's moral affinity with an age that has passed away. To compare a Corsican leader to the warrior heroes of Homer because of something so incidental as his watchdogs could only be comic unless there were in fact a Homeric dimension to his character as we perceive it.

Even when the way of direct allusion is denied him, Boswell manages continuously to surround his hero with the figures of classical myth and history. One of the stranger aspects of Paoli's character is his claim to second sight, in which the Corsicans universally believe. Boswell's appraisal, on the surface only a judicious weighing of the facts, finds means to introduce the appropriate parallels. It might be supposed, he says, that Paoli has promoted belief in his unusual talent "in order that he might have more authority in civilizing a rude and ferocious people, as Lycurgus pretended to have the sanction of the oracle at Delphos, as Numa gave it out that he had frequent interviews with the nymph Egeria, or as Marius persuaded the Romans that he received divine communications from a hind" (196). Yet one cannot believe, decides Boswell, that Paoli would descend to such pious frauds, and the case is straightway dismissed. But the case itself has been secondary, for what memory retains is the parallel in other respects with Lycurgus, Numa, and Marius, ancient civilizers of rude and ferocious peoples.

All Boswell's allusions to the ancient world are rooted in a strong context of personal impression, for the heroic dimension of Paoli's character, a quality which reveals itself primarily in his manner, is something that can only register on individual perception. Before we can accept the imaginative orientation that makes Paoli seem more a hero of antiquity than a man of the modern age, we must assent to Boswell's spontaneous response to this aura of greatness. At the center of Boswell's Plutarchan portrait is a perception that occurs with the intensity of a vision: "I had often enough formed the idea of a man continually such as I could conceive in my best moments. But this idea appeared like the ideas we are taught in the schools to form of things which may exist, but do not: of seas of milk and ships of amber. But I saw my highest idea realized in Paoli. It was impossible for me, speculate as I pleased, to have a little opinion of human nature in him" (188).

The very insubstantiality of the aura of greatness that surrounds Paoli suggests, however, the real meaning of the vision: it is not that Paoli has managed to recreate in real life the character of the imaginary hero but that Boswell, as he has come to know Paoli, has been insensibly drawn into the private and heroic world sustained by Paoli's imagination. Here again we are dealing with an idea of projected illusion so powerful as to have become a kind of alternative reality. This is the reality perceived by those who move in Paoli's presence, for what Paoli has found in his handbooks of greatness, in Plutarch and Livy, Boswell and the Corsicans discover in Paoli himself. The effect, as Boswell's talk of books and schools makes clear, is to undermine the idea of greatness as an abstraction and to rediscover it as an actual potentiality of human nature. Yet this in an unheroic age is a diminished potentiality, one which can express itself only in the manner and personality of the superior man.

There is in Boswell's Plutarchan portrait of Paoli a certain danger of excessive remoteness. Paoli's dream of the past, drawing substance from the imagined world of heroic antiquity, involves a stern image of heroism, one calculated to reveal him as someone singleminded, aloof, and hopelessly distant from his people and Boswell's audience. Boswell mitigates the sternness of the portrait in a manner that looks forward to his treatment of Johnson in the *Life*, presenting as counterpoint a side of Paoli's personality that appeals strongly to the benevolist ideal of the Good Man. As in the *Life*, the appeal is not directly to the theories of intrinsic moral sensibility advanced by writers like Shaftesbury, Hutcheson, and Butler, but to the simplified, popular, and somewhat sentimental version of those theories that was so strong an influence on eighteenth-century fiction and drama.

Paoli's benevolism is revealed in the way he deals with his role as governor of an unrealized commonwealth, symbolically analogous to the way a father deals with his children: he reproves wrongdoers, encourages rectitude, settles family disputes, and in general controls the tenor of Corsican life through a judicious bestowal of his approbation or disapproval. Each time Paoli appears in this paternal light, a submerged feudal metaphor informs the scene, for in the *Tour*, as often in eighteenth-century literature when we come across a benevolist character in a position of authority, an idea of romantic feudalism is in the background. But Paoli's benevolism is of course merged with the sterner demands of self-denial: "had he been a private gentleman, he probably would have married, and I am sure would have made as good a husband and father as he does a supreme magistrate and general. But his arduous and critical situation would not allow him to enjoy domestic felicity. He is wedded to his country, and the Corsicans are his children" (179). This symbolic relationship becomes the medium in which is dissolved the distance between the hero of antiquity and ordinary men.

Paoli's benevolism is thus embodied in the nature of his aspirations for Corsica as a state. The main objectives are peace, simplicity, and plenty, and when Boswell offers a studied compliment likening the "brave and free" Corsicans to the ancient Romans, he is quick to disavow the analogy: "he received my compliment very graciously, but observed that the Corsicans had no chance of being like the Romans, a great conquering nation who should extend its empire over half the globe. Their situation, and the modern political systems, rendered this impossible. 'But,' said he, 'Corsica may be a very happy country'" (171–72). If Paoli's response is a means of renouncing the rapacity of the modern European state, it involves too the renunciation of the ideal of leadership sanctioned by Boswell's Roman parallel. The feudal aspect of Paoli's relation to the Corsicans appears again in his devotion, as Corsica's leader, to the arts of peace: "he said the greatest happiness was not in glory but in goodness, and that Penn in his American colony, where he had established a people in quiet and contentment, was happier than Alexander the Great after destroying multitudes at the conquest of Thebes" (199).

Yet Paoli does not see himself as the governor of a feudal state, for as hero of the *Tour* he lives, as it were, inside the metaphor of romantic feudalism that controls Boswell's perception of Corsican society. Here again we sense the imaginative appeal of Paoli's dream of the past: Paoli has brought order out of anarchy in Corsica through the solitary force of his personality, and this, rather than any conscious effort on his part, has brought the Corsicans to recognize in their leader the actual personification of the state. Thus we see Paoli as a magistrate who, when he does not take his place in court, is in some sense revealed *as* the court: "he remained in his own apartment, and if any of those whose suits were determined by the sindacato were not pleased with the sentence they had an audience of Paoli, who never failed to convince them that justice had been done them. This appeared to me a necessary indulgence in the infancy of government. The Corsicans, having been so long in a state of anarchy, could not all at once submit their minds to the regular authority of justice. They would submit implicitly to Paoli, because they love and venerate him" (182). Only Paoli's strong personal presence behind the forms of government lends them validity in Corsican eyes, and we sense that if his presence were withdrawn Corsica would revert to anarchy and the forms would be swept away.

For Paoli, innocent of the sense in which his power derives from his own absorption in an imagined reality, this represents a purely practical problem. Since a bad man could in this situation become a tyrant, and since independent institutions are historically the best guard against despotism, the Corsicans must be brought to view government as something apart from the governing personality of a leader. Yet Paoli's measures in this direction, so apparently and hopefully practical, still reveal the essentially feudal and paternal nature of his relationship to his society: " 'our state,' said he, 'is young, and still requires the leading strings. I am desirous that the Corsicans should be taught to walk of themselves. Therefore when they come to me to ask whom they should choose for their Padre del Commune or other magis-trate, I tell them, "You know better than I do the able and honest men among your neighbours. Consider the consequence of your choice, not only to yourselves but to the island in general." In this manner I accustom them to feel their own importance as members of the state' " (175).

For the Corsicans, however, living within that magic sphere of illusion associated with Paoli's private dream of the heroic past, their leader is the state. A full revelation of Paoli's heroic gran-deur thus comes only when he drops his well-intentioned but somewhat theoretical attempts to dissociate himself from Corsica and speaks as the state. As when he deals with a Corsican turn-coat: " 'sir,' said he, 'Corsica makes it a rule to pardon the most unworthy of her children when they surrender themselves, even when they are forced to do so as is your case. You have now escaped. But take care. I shall have a strict eye upon you, and if ever you make the least attempt to return to your traitorous prac-tices, you know I can be avenged of you.' He spoke this with the fierceness of a lion, and from the awful darkness of his brow one could see that his thoughts of vengeance were terrible" (177). Behind such a scene lies the entire authority of Boswell's portrait of Paoli and the people he leads, for everything is concentrated at moments like this in the figure of the hero. The Corsica of the *Tour* is Paoli's creation, and even Boswell's feudal metaphor is insufficient to account for a situation where the external order that surrounds the hero is so completely identified with his mind and imagination.

This symbolic identification of Paoli with Corsica leaves both the leader and his people sadly vulnerable, and it is in the notion of vulnerability that we discover the final meaning of Boswell's story. On one level this is the vulnerability of a heroic leader and an idyllic state surrounded by the corrupt and threatening world of European duplicity. The *Tour* ends with Boswell, now safely in England, receiving from Paoli an account of the latest intrigue against him and Corsica: "as I passed by Bocagno, I learned that a disbanded Genoese officer was seeking associates to assassinate me. He could not succeed and, finding that he was discovered, he betook himself to the woods, where he has been slain" (215). This is the level on which eighteenth-century readers, taking the *Tour* as a story about political conflict, about oppression and the eternal struggle for natural liberty, made heroes of Paoli and the Corsicans.

At the same time, and on another level, the *Tour* is about the larger conflict of imagination and reality. For the mythic dimension of Boswell's portrayal of Paoli and his people involves a symbolic alignment of Corsica with the imaginary world of poetry and heroic legend, and of Europe with the dismayingly actual world of unheroic modernity. And eighteenth-century readers, looking to the *Tour* for confirmation of new doctrines of primitivism and natural liberty, undoubtedly responded to this as well, to the half-mythic vision of a Golden Age society governed by a hero out of Plutarch. Yet few, perhaps, would have perceived the sense in which Boswell's Corsica, besieged by the world of the unheroic and the unextraordinary, belongs wholly to the imagination, representing a reality transformed by a memory of the heroic past. The vulnerability of Paoli and Corsica is on this level the vulnerability of myth, or the power of myth to give shape to human existence, in a world increasingly dominated by the actual.

The vision of Corsica as a mythic state returns us therefore to Paoli, whose dream of the heroic past is at the heart of the process of imaginative transformation. For though Paoli and his people exist together within an illusion so strong as to have replaced a less satisfactory reality, Paoli is yet an isolated figure: the heroic world of Plutarch and the peaceful world of the Golden Age, though both are versions of the imagined past, are different worlds, and they merge in the *Tour* only because they stand together in symbolic opposition to the modern age. It is thus submerged tension between hero and milieu that gives meaning to our sense of Corsica as Paoli's creation, and though Boswell and the Corsicans are drawn partially into Paoli's dream of the past, they cannot inhabit it as he does. That dream is finally a private dream, the response of a heroic spirit to an age in which heroism seems to have disappeared, and behind it we glimpse the ultimate theme of spiritual isolation.

2

THE HERO & THE PAST

THE *TOUR*

TO THE HEBRIDES

TOWARD THE END of the *Tour to the Hebrides*, as Johnson's journey through the Highlands is drawing to an end, we see it already fading into the realm of memory. "He said to me often," Boswell reports, "that the time he spent in this Tour was the pleasantest part of his life, and asked me if I would lose the recollection of it for five hundred pounds. I answered I would not" (V.405). And in the *Life* itself we shall often find Johnson, in the midst of some period of personal suffering, looking back upon the tour as a kind of interlude in an otherwise painful existence: "the expedition to the Hebrides was the most pleasant journey that I ever made. Such an effort annually would give the world a little diversification'" (III.93–94). The *Tour* does in fact portray Johnson's journey as an interlude, giving us a hero who, in his travels through the primitive Highlands, is allowed temporarily to forget the misery of human existence.

Behind the bleaker mood of the *Life of Johnson* lies what we have called the principle of generic tension, symbolically representing Johnson, living spiritually apart from the eighteenth-century world he inhabits, as the image of the hero in an unheroic age. In the *Tour to the Hebrides*, which traces Johnson's journey out of the modern age and into a society still in touch with the remote and feudal past, this tension is partially resolved. The sense in which Johnson's Highland journey represents an escape into the past, and metaphorically an escape from self, is suggested by the passage from Johnson's *Journey to the Western Islands* which Boswell at one point introduces into his own narrative, a meditation on Iona, " 'whence savage clans and roving barbarians derived the benefits of knowledge, and the blessings of religion' ": " 'whatever withdraws us from the power of our senses, whatever makes the past, the distant, or the future, predominate over the present, advances us in the dignity of thinking beings' " (V.334).

The theme is ultimately one of spiritual release, and develops from an adjustment of the hero-milieu tension that normally gives shape to Boswellian narrative. For the *Tour to the Hebrides* is not about the hero in an unheroic world but about the hero as a stranger in a world where the heroic past still in some sense survives. Johnson's separation from his immediate milieu is thus represented in the *Tour* as a temporal distance, symbolically the distance between eighteenth-century England—specifically London, the image of the modern metropolis—and a remote and feudal past. This is an idea of the past which must be recaptured by, or recreated in, the imagination of a traveler from the modern age, and in this imaginative process, something not so far removed from dream or memory, lies the possibility of spiritual release. In Johnson we have the figure of the hero as traveler, journeying through regions that lie somewhere between past and present, and somewhere beyond the misery of normal existence.

This relationship between hero and setting determines the special atmosphere of the *Tour to the Hebrides*, for as the affinities of the *Tour to Corsica* are with pastoral, and those of the *Life of Johnson* with formal tragedy, the *Tour* resembles comic romance. The resemblance was not lost on contemporary readers: "Dr. Johnson and Mr. Boswell," wrote a correspondent of the *Gentleman's Magazine* in 1785, "seem the most agreeable associates that ever travelled together since the renowned Knight of La Mancha and his incomparable 'Squire.' "[1] The principle of

generic tension is most often found in comic literature, in bur-
lesque or mock-epic or comic romance. In Boswell, though we
are aware of its comic influence in certain scenes of the *Life*, the
same principle becomes a metaphor for the spiritual isolation of
a great man, and it is only in the *Tour to the Hebrides*, where the
isolation of the hero is for a time forgotten, that the more innocent concerns of comedy wholly emerge.

In the short character sketch of Johnson which comes close to
the beginning of the *Tour*, Boswell describes his hero as "prone
to supersitition, but not to credulity. Though his imagination
might incline him to a belief of the marvelous, and the mysterious,
his vigorous reason examined the evidence with jealousy" (V.17–
18). The *Tour* is in one aspect about this tension between reason
and imagination. Reason, in Boswell's sense, is represented in the
usual tone of Johnson's conversation in the *Tour*; an exclusive
emphasis on scenes that show Johnson jealously examining the
evidence must lead to something like Frank Brady's interesting
conclusion that "the *Tour* is antiromance."[2] Imagination, involving associations with the marvelous and the mysterious, is fulfilled
in the *Tour* by the strangeness of Highland scenes and by a journey motif that imitates comic romance. Johnson's Highland journey is not simply an escape into the past but into a setting where
reason and imagination are no longer seriously in conflict: "in
the presence of extraordinary actuality," Wallace Stevens says,
"consciousness takes the place of imagination."

The distant past is represented in the landscape of the *Tour* by
the physical remains that native tradition associates with the days
of the Norse invasions. Neither Boswell nor Johnson has any patience with the occasional assertion that the Norsemen have not
been absorbed by the populace—"he told us, there was a colony
of Danes in his parish; that they had landed at a remote period of
time, and still remained a distinct people" (V.70–71)—but actual
reminders of their presence are everywhere. In the towers where
the inhabitants withdrew in time of siege, the caves where stores

of food were hidden, in the primitive monuments of early Christianity and occasional suggestions of an earlier pagan worship, the travelers are surrounded by reminders of the remote past. Johnson's vigorous reason is always motivating him to strict inquiry and a jealous examination of the evidence, but we seldom lose our sense of the presence of the past, of the traveler moving through a region whose real history survives now only as credulous tradition.

History is present, too, in the ruined cathedrals that remain as reminders of a medieval Christianity which consistently appeals to Johnson's emotions. In many of the ruins Johnson sees only the symbols of a faith now decayed and is moved to a kind of sad piety, but those he associates with Knox's Reformation draw his anger: "I happened to ask where John Knox was buried. Dr. Johnson burst out, 'I hope in the highway. I have been looking at his reformations'" (V.61). Knox's mob embodies for Johnson the evil of what he would have called democratical notions, present in his world in movements of the "Wilkes and Liberty" variety, and Knox's religion represents that enthusiasm he defined in the *Dictionary* as "a vain belief of private revelation" and "heat of imagination; violence of passion; confidence of opinion": "Dr. Johnson seemed quite wrapt up in the contemplation of the scenes which were now presented to him. He kept his hat off while he was upon any part of the ground where the cathedral had stood. He said well, that 'Knox had set on a mob, without knowing where it would end; and that differing from a man in doctrine was no reason why you should pull his house about his ears.' As we walked in the cloisters, there was a solemn echo, while he talked loudly of a proper retirement from the world" (V.62). The mood of melancholy contemplation in such scenes is in a sense destroyed by the intrusion of the present.

The great event in the historical background of the Tour is not so remote as the Norse invasions or Knox's Reformation. The rising of the clans in 1745, the last great attempt to place

Charles Edward on the throne of England, was recent history, and a symbol of the kind of romance that always attaches to heroic failure. Only the readers of such fictional accounts as Scott's *Waverley* can now perhaps recover any sense of the '45 as an event more out of myth and romance than out of political history, dealing more with such archetypal themes as the return of the exiled king than with the relative merits of the Stuart or the Hanoverian claim to the throne. Boswell's own response to the rebellion provides the measure of its romantic appeal, as when he hears a Highlander describe the course of events that led up to Culloden: "as he narrated the particulars of that ill-advised, but brave attempt, I could not refrain from tears. . . . The very Highland names, or the sound of a bagpipe, will stir my blood, and fill me with . . . a crowd of sensations with which sober rationality has nothing to do" (V.140).

We are everywhere reminded of the '45 in the *Tour*, for the actors in the story are still alive, and the old sentiments linger. Johnson's meeting with Flora Macdonald, who played a heroic part in Prince Charles's escape, becomes the excuse for Boswell's narrative of the episode, a kind of synecdoche for the romantic aspect of the Jacobite theme. Again, we glimpse the emotional quality of Johnson's response not in his conversation but in certain moments of dramatic implication: "while the punch went round, Dr. Johnson kept a close whispering conference with Mrs. M'Kinnon, which, however, was loud enough to let us hear that the subject of it was the particulars of Prince Charles's escape" (V.264); "Dr. Johnson's bed was the very bed in which the grandson of the unfortunate King James the Second lay, on one of the nights after the failure of his rash attempt in 1745–6, while he was eluding the pursuit of the emissaries of government. . . . To see Dr. Samuel Johnson lying in that bed, in the isle of Sky, in the house of Miss Flora Macdonald, struck me with such a group of ideas as it is not easy for words to describe, as they passed through the mind" (V.185–86).

If the '45 has passed away into myth, however, the impact of
the defeat at Culloden is still visible. In 1745 and 1715 the Highland clans had provided the exiled Stuarts with the greater part
of the Jacobite armies, and in 1746 the English government
mounted its first successful attack on the clan relationship itself.
The Highlands were disarmed, the tartans, the outward symbol
of clan allegiance, were forbidden to be worn, and the heritable
jurisdictions of the chiefs, in which they exercised absolute political and legal authority over their followers, were abolished.
As Johnson and Boswell travel through the Hebrides, an ancient
feudal society is in the process of dissolution, and the Scottish
Highlands are being drawn, slowly and inevitably, into a modern
world from which they had maintained an almost complete cultural independence.

In Johnson's response to this state of affairs, there is the same
strong tension between imagination and reason. As a rational
observer Johnson is quick to refute Boswell's contention that
"mankind were happier in the feudal state of subordination, than
they are in the modern state of independency": "*Johnson.* 'To
be sure, the *Chief* was: but we must think of the number of individuals. That *they* were less happy, seems plain; for that state
from which all escape as soon as they can, and to which none
return after they have left it, must be less happy; and this is the
case with the state of dependance on a chief or great man'"
(V.106). Johnson does recognize that the abolition of heritable
jurisdictions has left a vacuum of authority, especially in the
multitude of social issues that are not strictly actionable at law;
but his comments even on this apparent evil are those of the
rational observer doing his best to remain objective and to weigh
the available evidence.

Yet feudalism, in a world grown unheroic and commercial,
represents a social ideal of primitive virtue and hard simplicity
with a strong emotional attraction for Johnson, and the hero's
imaginative response works counter to the objective and rational

examination of the ancient state of subordination that typically
emerges in his conversation. "It affords a generous and manly
pleasure," Johnson said in his *Journey to the Western Islands*,
"to conceive a little nation gathering its fruits and tending its
herds with fearless confidence, though it lies open on every side
to invasion, where, in contempt of walls and trenches, every
man sleeps securely with his sword beside him; where all on the
first approach of hostility come together at the call to battle, as
at a summons to a festal show . . . to lose this spirit, is to lose what
no small advantage will compensate." It is to just such an imaginative conception that Johnson's emotions respond in the *Tour*.

The symbol of the feudal relationship is Raasay, a kind of
locus amoenus for the parts of the *Tour* that deal with the old
order. "Rasay and I took a walk," says Boswell at one point, "and
had some cordial conversation. I conceived a more than ordinary
regard for this worthy gentleman. His family has possessed this
island above four hundred years. It is the remains of the estate of
Macleod of Lewis, whom he represents.—When we returned,
Dr. Johnson walked with us to see the old chapel. He was in fine
spirits. He said, 'This is truly the patriarchal life: this is what we
came to find' " (V.167). What Johnson and Boswell are seeing
of course is not the patriarchal life but a semblance of it that has
survived the abolition of the heritable jurisdictions. The sign of
Rasay's adaptability is the voluntary allegiance of his people; his
lands "do not altogether yield him a very large revenue: and yet
he lives in great splendour; and so far is he from distressing his
people that, in the present rage for emigration, not a man has left
his estate" (V.165).

In such a setting, nostalgia for a nonexistent past may safely be
indulged by even the most vigorously rational traveler, for the
possible evils of the feudal state have been abolished, and the old
order survives merely in sentiment and tradition. Johnson's imaginative response is personal and philosophical, not political, the
same sort of response as we are expected to have to a poet's pic-

ture of a land of pastoral or romance, or of the irrecoverable Golden Age. In truth Raasay represents an ideal of simplified civilization rather than of primitive feudalism: the chief is "a sensible, polite, and most hospitable gentleman," his reception of Boswell and Johnson is gracious and unreservedly courteous, his household is well-ordered and his family cultivated. But in his relation to his clansmen, and his respect for old sentiments and traditions, we see the leader, stripped of his authority, who refuses to be debased by his loss of power into that villain of the commercial age, a rapacious, rackrenting landlord.

The symbol of such debasement is Armidale in Skye. Sir Alexander Macdonald, an English-bred chieftain, embodies all that is bad about a spiritual break with the past. The travelers' reception is a sorry reverse of that they got at Raasay, for Sir Alexander is stingy and his hospitality is grudging, narrow, and mean spirited. Macdonald's purely commercial relationship with his clansmen, who have become the hardpressed tenants of an unproductive estate and who have responded by fleeing in increasing numbers to America, draws from Johnson his most spirited defense of "the patriarchal life": "*Johnson.* 'Were I in your place, sir, in seven years I would make this an independent island. I would roast oxen whole, and hang out a flag as a signal to the Macdonalds to come and get beef and whiskey.'—Sir Alexander was still starting difficulties.—*Johnson.* 'Nay, sir; if you are born to object, I have done with you. Sir, I would have a magazine of arms.'— *Sir Alexander.* 'They would rust.'—*Johnson.* 'Let there be men to keep them clean. Your ancestors did not use to let their arms rust'" (V.151).

Armidale represents the evil of a society where money replaces human values. Here at last is a Highland question that involves no problematic conflict of reason and imagination, for in the dissolution of Highland society through enforced emigration Johnson sees the sacrifice of the old order to callous commercial motives. Emigration is a constant theme in the *Tour*, its absence a sign that portions of Highland society, through the efforts of a good chief, have survived the transition to modernity unharmed (as when we are told that Rasay has lost not a single one of his people), its presence a sad picture of dissolution: "in the morning I walked out, and saw a ship, the Margaret of Clyde, pass by with a number of emigrants on board. It was a melancholy sight"; "we reached the harbour of Portree, in Sky, which is a large and good one. There was lying in it a vessel to carry off the emigrants, called the Nestor. It made a short settlement of the differences of a chief and his clan."

In Johnson's eyes the greed of the chiefs has resulted in the final degradation of the emigrants: "to a man of mere animal life, you can urge no argument against going to America, but that it may be some time before he will get the earth to produce. But a man of any intellectual enjoyment will not easily go and immerse himself and his posterity for ages in barbarism" (V.78). But even barbarism is preferable to a hard existence on a Highland farm, working for a bare subsistence in the face of steadily escalating rents, and Johnson's wrath is ultimately turned against the chiefs who have totally abandoned their feudal responsibilities: "after dinner, M'Queen sat by us a while, and talked with us. He said, all the Laird of Glenmorison's people would bleed for him, if they were well used; but that seventy men had gone out of the Glen to America. That he himself intended to go next year; for that the rent of his farm, which twenty years ago was only five pounds, was now raised to twenty pounds. That he could pay ten pounds, and live; but no more.—Dr. Johnson said, he wished M'Queen laird of Glenmorison, and the laird to go to America" (V.136–37).

The theme of emigration reveals the sense in which the tension between reason and imagination in Johnson's personality, involving a problematic conflict between present and past, is occasionally resolved. For reason suggests that chieftains as rapacious as Macdonald and Glenmorison are harming both their people and themselves through their callous commercialism, and imagination retreats sympathetically to the idea of a feudal state where arms were not allowed to rust and where clansmen were ready to die for their leader. The solution is represented in Raasay, where the past merges with the present, where the laird is a civilized man with a proper respect for the tradition he has inherited, and where his people repay him with a modern version of the old feudal allegiance. Raasay represents the proper union of the historical past and the changing present, a social context in which past and present enrich each other. Yet the same tension is in another sense resolved in the character of the hero as traveler, a combination of the severe rationalist and a more romantic and emotional observer who discovers in what he calls the system of insular life powerful reminders of an age simpler and more heroic than his own.

TWO

If a strong sense of the historical past haunts the landscape of the *Tour*, there is also a sense in which the present reality of Hebridean life *is* the past. Johnson and he have been drawn to the Hebrides, Boswell tells us, from "a notion that we might there contemplate a system of life almost totally different from what we had been accustomed to see; and, to find simplicity and wildness, and all the circumstances of a remote time or place, so near to our native great island, was an object within the reach of reasonable curiosity" (V.13). The expectation of strangeness, of the unfamiliar and even the marvelous, aligns the *Tour* with romance, making Johnson's journey through the Hebrides a metaphor of escape from self. One again recalls the London of Boswell's *Life of Johnson*, where life is busy, complicated, and savagely modern. The *Tour*, in its movement toward scenes of simplicity and wildness, toward the circumstances of a remote time and place, represents (among other things) the hero's symbolic escape from that world of modern strife.

For both travelers the wildness of nature in the Hebrides serves mainly to deepen this sense of cultural and temporal distance, for there is little in their attitude that reveals the growing interest of their age in the more awesome aspects of natural scenery, in those suggestions of vastness, power, magnificence or infinitude that Burke and Gerard saw as the basis of the sublime. Boswell and his hero respond always to the contrast between their own familiar world and the strangeness of Highland life and scenery, an emphasis distinctly contemplative. The familiarity of the scene alone is what leads Johnson at one point to refuse a tour of a cultivated nobleman's well-laid-out domain: "he always said, that he was not come to Scotland to see fine places, of which there were enough in England; but wild objects,—mountains,—waterfalls,—peculiar manners; in short, things which he had not seen before" (V.112).

As always Johnson is the philosophical observer, and the colorless neutrality of his terms—"wild objects," "peculiar manners"—disguises the degree to which the journey through the Hebrides is actually a movement into the past. But the *Tour* is Boswell's narrative, and the complex suggestiveness of his description again and again places the hero against a background close to romance: "our boatmen sung with great spirit. Dr. Johnson observed, that naval musick was very ancient. As we came near the shore, the singing of our rowers was succeeded by that of reapers, who were busy at work, and who seemed to shout as much as to sing, while they worked with a bounding activity. Just as we landed, I observed a cross, or rather the ruins of one, upon a rock, which had to me a pleasing vestige of religion. I perceived a large company coming out from the house. We met them as we walked up" (V.165). The rowers sing, the reapers chant, the scene merges with the life of a time long past, and even as they observe, takes on the timelessness of a memory or a dream.

The barren moors and rugged coastlines of the Hebrides are the "romantick scene" which is the background of the *Tour*, but the scene is dominated by the castles between which the travelers move on their journey. Gazing on these piles, one is moved insensibly to thoughts of the past: "the old tower must be of great antiquity. There is a drawbridge,—what has been a moat,—and an ancient court. . . . The thickness of the walls, the small slaunting windows, and a great iron door at the entrance on the second story as you ascend the stairs, all indicate the rude times in which this castle was erected" (V.119–20). Or a Highland castle "built quite upon the shore," looking out at the water that brought the barbarian invaders, gives a sense of migratory space: "the windows look upon the main ocean, and the King of Denmark is Lord Errol's nearest neighbour on the north-east" (V.100). Though such castles are, like the cathedral ruins of the *Tour*, monuments of a primitive past, they do not suggest specific historical associations so much as the vague and general impression of a remote time.

Between the castles is the rough countryside, peopled only by simple peasants who live in rude huts, and provided only occasionally with a wretched inn. Johnson and Boswell discover true hospitality only when they are entertained in private houses, and in such houses they again often find themselves in the midst of a timeless scene: "we here enjoyed the comfort of a table plentifully furnished, the satisfaction of which was heightened by a numerous and cheerful company; and we for the first time had a specimen of the joyous social manners of the inhabitants of the Highlands. They talked in their own ancient language, with fluent vivacity, and sung many Erse songs" (V.157). The Erse songs, and the simplicity of the diversion, are such as have been devised by a people shut off for ages from the outside world, and we have a sense of Johnson and Boswell as visitors from a different age. Ignorant of the language and content to observe, they gaze upon the scene as a tableau of older times.

The atmosphere of romance becomes most real, however, when Johnson and Boswell come in contact with the supernatural, and in a manner that suspends all questions about superstition and rational belief. Almost every Highlander, on whatever level of society or education, harbors some belief in the second sight (except the ministers, who have a professional interest in dispelling it): "an old woman, who was in the house, said one day, 'M'Quarrie will be at home to-morrow, and will bring two gentlemen with him'; and she said, she saw his servant return in red and green. He did come home the next day. He had two gentlemen with him; and his servant had a new red and green livery, which M'Quarrie had bought for him at Edinburgh. . . . This, he assured us, was a true story" (V.320). Such conviction neutralizes the scepticism of the rationalist, for whether or not the second sight is real is unimportant: *belief* in it is real, and the customs and manners and even the perception of the Highlanders are governed by a routine contact with the supernatural.

For magic is real when the members of a society accept it as such, reality being a matter of belief and perception. (In the seventeenth century, the great age of witchcraft trials, there were those who pled guilty to the charge of necromancy, not because they were mad or weak-willed or tortured into the admission but because they *were* witches, dealing with the powers of darkness in a world where those powers were as real as the atom is in ours.) In the Hebrides the modern traveler is moving through a world where magic is still at work and where supernatural considerations strongly influence the attitudes and everyday behavior of the people. The society in which magic is at work calls for a suspension of disbelief on the part of the outside observer, who has no power to refute the total phenomenon of belief.

In the *Tour* the persistence of local superstition heightens the atmosphere of romance, for it is in that genre of literature that we most often discover a world where magic is as real as the rocks and trees of the landscape. In this too, Johnson and Boswell have taken a journey backward in time, for a society that believes in the supernatural is wholly untouched by the modern tendency toward rational and scientific scepticism, and lives on as an isolated colony of the forgotten primitive world. In the Hebrides the marvelous is everywhere and is not marvelous. The sight of a Highland lake, for instance, brings forth an item of local history concerning "a sea-horse, which came and devoured a man's daughter." The man builds a fire and roasts a sow, hoping the smell will bring the monster out of the lake: "in the fire was put a spit. The man lay concealed behind a low wall of loose stones, and he had an avenue formed for the monster, with two rows of large flat stones, which extended from the fire over the summit of the hill, till it reached the side of the loch. The monster came, and the man with the red-hot spit destroyed it. Malcolm shewed me the little hiding-place, and the rows of stones. He did not laugh when he told this story" (V.171).

Moving among people who hold such beliefs, Boswell and Johnson are in the world of ballad and song, where witches and monsters and ghosts are a matter of everyday reality, or at least of the common traditions that form the cultural memory of a society and that determine their attitudes toward the external world. The "system of insular life" that the travelers have come to observe is only partly a system of social relationships and economic facts. For the rest, a system of beliefs that includes magic and fabulous tradition, rational comparison with modern society is impossible, and they are left free to respond imaginatively to an atmosphere of strangeness and romance.

Through the Highlands the "romantick scene"—landscape, ruins, wild nature, fabulous tradition—is in a sense a backdrop to Johnson and Boswell's actual journey. In the Hebrides, where frequent storms make voyage by sea impossible, the travelers repeatedly find themselves the unwilling members of a society where life goes on as usual—"the weather was worse than yesterday. I felt as if imprisoned." The rhythm of bad weather and inhibited movement dominates the latter part of the *Tour,* and their involuntary confinement is responsible both for Johnson's occasional fretfulness and for much of his best conversation: "it was a very wet stormy day; we were therefore obligated to remain here, it being impossible to cross the sea to Rasay"; "there was this day the most terrible storm of wind and rain that I ever remember. It made such an awful impression on us all, as to produce, for some time, a kind of dismal quietness in the house. The day was passed without much conversation"; "there was as great a storm of wind and rain as I have almost ever seen, which necessarily confined us to the house; but we were fully compensated by Dr. Johnson's conversation."

The frequency of wind and rain and the difficulty of travel, however, eventually merge with the travelers' sense of personal adventure and of the Highlands as the landscape of romance. Boswell and Johnson are urban dwellers, and men in cities quickly lose that sense of man's dependence on nature that is common in wilder regions. In the Hebrides the brute force of nature is a fact larger than human existence, especially an existence so precariously won from an unpromising landscape, and man is always subject to the elements. In such a situation one's thoughts inevitably move backward to a time when all human existence was precarious. But there is a certain imaginative appeal involved, for this too is the context of romance, where a single hero ventures from the warmth and safety of the castle into a forbidding landscape. As I have observed earlier, one is often reminded during the Hebridean stage of the narrative of a passage from Johnson's own *Journey:*

> The fictions of the Gothick romances were not so remote from credibility as they are now thought. In the full prevalence of the feudal institution, when violence desolated the world, and every baron lived in a fortress, forests and castles were regularly succeeded by each other, and the adventurer might very suddenly pass from the gloom of woods, or the ruggedness of moors, to seats of plenty, gaiety, and magnifi-

cence. Whatever is imaged in the wildest tale, if giants, dragons, and enchantment be excepted, would be felt by him who, wandering in the mountains without a guide, or upon the sea without a pilot, should be carried amidst his terror and uncertainty, to the hospitality and elegance of *Raasay* or *Dunvegan.*

In the *Tour*, though the world is no longer desolated by violence, and giants, dragons, and enchantment persist only in the traditions of the inhabitants, the landscape is still forbidding and nature violent, and shelter and society take on a special value. For Johnson especially, whose view of existence takes full account of civilized comforts and everyday amenities, the contrast is exhilarating. When one may dine any evening with friends, the warmth and light and conversation available at the Mitre or the Turk's Head are to be taken for granted, but to discover them in the Hebrides, amidst the rude mountains and the violence of the elements, is to rediscover their full value: "our entertainment here was in so elegant a style, and reminded my fellow-traveller so much of England, that he became quite joyous. He laughed, and said, 'Boswell, we came in at the wrong end of this island.'— 'Sir, (said I,) it was best to keep this for the last.'—He answered, 'I would have it both first and last'" (V.208).

The appeal of the Highland journey is in large part one of release, a chance to lose the consciousness of the present in impressions of the past. The mood of the *Tour* as a whole supports Boswell's occasional impulse to identify his present freedom from care with the scenes that surround him, rather than with his pleasure in contemplating those scenes: "they dance here every night. The queen of our ball was the eldest Miss Macleod, of Rasay, an elegant well-bred woman, and celebrated for her beauty over all these regions, by the name of Miss Flora Rasay. There seemed to be no jealousy, no discontent among them; and the gaiety of the scene was such, that I for a moment doubted whether unhappiness had any place in Rasay" (V.179). This again is close to romance: the vision of pastoral innocence, of simplicity and

gaiety and plenty in a natural setting, has always been a fiction
created by the civilized mind to answer its own psychological
needs, an imaginary world free from the complexities, pressures,
and disappointments of ordinary life.

But the vision is only a vision, and Boswell immediately revises
it: "my delusion was soon dispelled, by recollecting the following
lines of my fellow-traveler: 'Hope not life from pain or danger
free, / Or think the doom of man revers'd for thee!' " Yet Johnson as hero of the *Tour to the Hebrides* is a Johnson far removed
from the stern moralist of "The Vanity of Human Wishes," a
traveler who, succumbing in part to the imaginative appeal of
new surroundings, does for a time forget the misery of human
existence. Again one thinks of the *Life of Johnson*, where Johnson's isolation is preeminently the isolation of the hero in an unheroic world. Life in the Hebrides, though finally representing a
sphere of reality that remains alien to a visitor from the modern
age, represents at the same time a forgotten world of romance,
magic, and primitive simplicity that exists as a temporary refuge
for a mind in heroic conflict with the modern age.

THREE

There is in Boswell's portrayal of Johnson in the *Tour to the
Hebrides* a certain basic counterpoint of public and private per-
spectives, similar to that "oscillation between public and private
views of Johnson" which David Passler has correctly identified
in the *Life*.[3] In the public perspective, as in many scenes of the
Life, we are looking at Johnson as a character surrounded by the
actual, by horses and books and teacups and, preeminently, people. This is a portrayal of the hero nearly swallowed up, as it
were, by his milieu, and it leads in the direction of simplification
bordering on (affectionate) caricature. Boswell's character sketch
of Johnson at the beginning of the *Tour* may be taken as an ab-

stract of this view: it contains a section on Johnson's beliefs: "he was a sincere and zealous christian, of high church of England and monarchical principles"; one on his physical appearance: "he wore boots, and a very wide brown cloth coat, with pockets which might almost have held the two volumes of his folio dictionary"; and one with special significance for the *Tour* as travel narrative: 'like the ancient Greeks and Romans, he allowed himself to look upon all other nations but his own as barbarians. . . . He was indeed, if I may be allowed the phrase, at bottom much of a *John Bull*, much of a blunt *true born Englishman.* There was a stratum of common clay under the rock of marble" (V.16–19).

As when he deals with Johnson's eccentricities in the *Life*, Boswell is here presenting a view of the hero as he appears not on the higher level of inward spiritual conflict but on the lower level of his milieu, of his society and age. To view Johnson exclusively on this level, as a creature of the eighteenth century as Boswell portrays it, is to see him as something of a humor character, someone belonging to that large company of imaginary figures we associate with Fielding and Smollett and Sterne, with Hogarth or—in the case of his illustrations for the *Tour*—Thomas Rowlandson. In both the *Tour* and the *Life* Boswell is continuously poking gentle fun at this view, exposing its limitations even as he presents it and emphasizing it initially only because it contains an essential truth about Johnson's anomalous relation to his world. The public perspective on Johnson is always offered as less a comment on Johnson than on his public.

In the *Tour to the Hebrides*, however, the notion of Johnson as something close to a humor character has a special significance, for Boswell's appeal is specifically to the eighteenth-century character of the English traveler, a kind of sturdy provincial who carries solid English values with him into strange societies. The character appears in fiction as the typical Defoe hero or heroine, resolutely English and bourgeois among all foreign distractions— or even, as in *Robinson Crusoe*, in solitude—and it can be seen to influence, to one degree or another, much eighteenth-century travel literature, from *Roderick Random* to *Voyage to Lisbon*. Thus the Johnson of the *Life*, whose orthodoxy and Toryism are major elements in his conflict with the age, can appear in the *Tour* as a sincere and zealous Christian, a blunt trueborn Englishman.

When Johnson appears in this light, we are again aware of his Highland journey as primarily an interlude in a life of grave moral conflict, and of the *Tour* as a narrative in some respects close to comic romance. For Johnson the trueborn Englishman is, in his transit over the Caledonian hemisphere, a kind of Don Quixote issued forth from the gates of eighteenth-century London. This represents a view of Johnson's identification with London that is at once comic and serious; London is civilization, and the movement of the *Tour* is away from civilization, off through a wild and romantic landscape and back to civilization again. Though we never see Johnson actually in London, the city is established early as both a cultural symbol and the representative milieu of the hero: "I doubted that it would not be possible to prevail on Dr. Johnson to relinquish, for some time, the felicity of a London life, which, to a man who can enjoy it with full intellectual relish, is apt to make existence in any narrower sphere seem insipid or irksome. I doubted that he would not be willing to come down from his elevated state of philosophical dignity; from a superiority of wisdom among the wise, and of learning among the learned; and from flashing his wit upon minds bright enough to reflect it" (V.14).

London, that is, as spiritual milieu. But Johnson's movement away from London is also a temporary movement away from the self that is identified with London, an aspect of the journey that Boswell continuously emphasizes: "as I saw him now for the first time on horseback, jaunting about at his ease in quest of pleasure and novelty, the very different occupations of his former laborious life, his admirable productions, his *London*, his *Rambler*, etc. etc. immediately presented themselves to my mind, and the contrast made a strong impression on my imagination" (V.132). Johnson's initial resistance to travel—" 'if we must ride much, we shall not go; and there's an end on't' "—gives way to a sense of the tour as personal adventure—"as we sailed along by moonlight, in a sea somewhat rough, and often between black and gloomy rocks, Dr. Johnson said, 'If this is not *roving among the Hebrides*, nothing is' " (V.333)—and to a joyous sense of its contrast with his familiar and public role at the center of London life: "after we were out of the shelter of Scalpa, and in the sound between it and Rasay, which extended about a league, the wind made the sea very rough. I did not like it.—*Johnson.* 'This now is the Atlantick. If I should tell at a tea table in London, that I have crossed the Atlantick in an open boat, how they'd shudder, and what a fool they'd think me to expose myself to such danger!' " (V.163).

Johnson's journey through the wild landscape of the Hebrides is also a journey backward into youth. In the *Life*, after a certain point, we seldom see a day when Johnson is without continuous physical pain, but in a setting where time seems to have stopped, the relentless chronology of advancing years becomes irrelevant, and Johnson's recovery of energy becomes a conscious denial of old age: "during the whole of our Tour he shewed uncommon spirit, could not bear to be treated like an old or infirm man . . . insomuch that, at our landing at Icolmkill, when Sir Allan M'Lean and I submitted to be carried on men's shoulders from the boat to shore, as it could not be brought quite close to land, he sprang into the sea, and waded vigorously out" (V.368); "I changed my clothes in part, and was at pains to get myself well dried. Dr. Johnson resolutely kept on all his clothes, wet as they were, letting them steam before the smoky turf fire. I thought him in the wrong; but his firmness was, perhaps, a species of heroism" (V.345). Johnson emerges from the *Tour* as a man who has undergone a rejuvenation of spirit, who has come to see his journey

as a period in which the dreaded onset of old age and infirmity
has for a time been reversed.

At the same time, Boswell's identification of his hero with
London is a central element in what might be called a comedy of
nonrecognition, something that again takes us into the sphere
of comic romance. In London, Johnson is the center of a circle of
famous men, "the gay, the ingenious, and the great," and everyone from the King to the literate tradesman knows his accomp-
lishments and his character. "Dr. Samuel Johnson's character,"
said Boswell at the beginning of his sketch, "religious, moral,
political and literary, nay his figure and manner, are, I believe,
more generally known than those of almost any man" (V.16).
But in the Hebrides, among ignorant and provincial and usually
illiterate people, any impression Johnson makes depends on his
powers of mind and personality. This theme, of the philosopher
among peasants, becomes a continuous comic motif: "the landlady said to me, 'Is not this the great Doctor that is going about
through the country?'—I said, 'Yes.'—'Ay, (said she,) we heard
of him. I made an errand into the room on purpose to see him. . . .
If I had thought of it, I would have shewn him a child of mine,
who has had a lump on his throat for some time.'—'But, (said I,)
he is not a doctor of physick.' 'Is he an oculist?' said the landlord.—'No, (said I,) he is only a very learned man' " (V.96).

By and large, the philosopher wins out. We sense, before we
are very far along in the *Tour*, that Johnson is going to leave a
legend behind him when he departs from the Hebrides and heads
once again for London. But there is still the problem of what one
does with a philosopher once one has him, a variation in the
comedy of nonrecognition: "Hay led the horse's head, talking to
Dr. Johnson as much as he could; and (having heard him, in the
forenoon, express a pastoral pleasure on seeing the goats browz-
ing) just when the Doctor was uttering his displeasure, the fellow cried, with a very Highland accent, 'See, such pretty goats!'
Then he whistled, *whu!* and made them jump.—Little did he con-

ceive what Doctor Johnson was. Here now was a common ignorant Highland clown imagining that he could divert, as one does
a child,—*Dr. Samuel Johnson*" (V.144).

Or Johnston. The final scene in the comedy is provided not by
a common ignorant Highland clown but by the chieftain Lochbuy. In a contest of provincialisms, Lochbuy would have a certain advantage over Dickens's Podsnap, for England, in the
chieftain's world, does not exist. Lochbuy has been described to
the travelers both as a Don Quixote and "a great roaring bragga-
docio, a kind of Sir John Falstaff," but "the truth is, that Lochbuy
proved to be only a bluff, comely, noisy old gentleman, proud
of his hereditary consequence, and a very hearty and hospitable
landlord. . . . Being told that Dr. Johnson did not hear well, Lochbuy bawled out to him, 'Are you of the Johnstons of Glencro, or
of Ardnamurchan?'—Dr. Johnson gave him a significant look,
but made no answer; and I told Lochbuy that he was not John-
ston, but John*son*, and that he was an Englishman" (V.341).

Eventually, however, our more serious sense of the total impression Johnson is making on the Highlanders reminds us that
these scenes of nonrecognition are only a leitmotif in a grander
movement that is to reveal Johnson the traveler as a genuinely
great man. As always in Boswellian narrative, this is partly a
question of the hero's manner—"there's something great in his
appearance," said the landlady back at Ellon—but it primarily
concerns the impact of Johnson's conversation. For in his journey
through the Highlands, passing among people who know little
philosophy or literature, Johnson recreates through the quality
of his conversation the persona of *Rasselas* and the *Rambler*, and
it is to catch the Rambler (as Boswell calls him throughout) in
his new surroundings that Boswell so often emphasizes the external scene. At times, in fact, the setting becomes nearly as important as the hero.

This external view of Johnson, in some sense inseparable from
what we have called public perspective, is among other things a

mode of psychological exploration. In the *Life of Johnson*, for instance, we see Johnson's tendency to abstraction and self-absorption in those moments when he picks up a book and reads in company, or where he detaches himself from conversation and goes to stare out a window. Boswell dramatizes this same aspect of his hero's personality in the *Tour* simply by locating Johnson in an external scene: "Dr. Johnson placed himself on the ground, with his back against a large fragment of rock. The wind being high, he let down the cocks of his hat, and tied it with his handkerchief under his chin. While we were employed in examining the stone . . . he amused himself with reading *Gataker on Lots and on the Christian Watch*, a very learned book, of the last age. . . . When we descried him from above, he had a most eremitical appearance; and on our return told us he had been so much engaged by Gataker, that he never missed us" (V.302).

In such scenes details that merely suggest the wildness of the setting pursue the symbolic contrast between the rough landscape of the Hebrides and the tamed civilization of London. Usually the figure of Johnson dominates the landscape, as Saint Paul's church would dominate the windswept moors of the Highlands. When the setting dominates, however, the idea of the journey as escape and adventure reemerges. In such moments our sense of the strangeness of the scene becomes the measure of Johnson's response: "the wind had now risen pretty high, and was against us; but we had four stout rowers, particularly a Macleod, a robust, black-haired fellow, half-naked, and bare-headed, something between a wild Indian and an English tar. Dr. Johnson sat high on the stern, like a magnificent Triton. Malcolm sung an Erse song, the chorus of which was '*Hatyin foam foam eri*'. . . . The boatmen and Mr. M'Queen chorused, and all went well" (V.162); "we had many showers, and it soon grew pretty dark. Dr. Johnson sat silent and patient. Once he said, as he looked on the black coast of Sky,—black, as being composed of rocks seen in the dusk,—'This is very solemn' " (V.257).

Simply by giving such importance to the external scene, Boswell is suggesting the degree to which the journey is absorbing the psychic energies that in Johnson's London existence are used up in internal conflict. Many pages of the *Life* are taken up, for instance, with discussion of Johnson's fear of death; with, indeed, his discomfort at almost any reminder of mortality. In the more relaxed atmosphere of the *Tour*, this same side of Johnson's personality emerges only in isolated scenes, as glimpses of the life of suffering from which the hero as traveler has temporarily escaped. As when he enters an unroofed chapel with human bones lying aboveground: "Dr. Johnson would not look at the bones. He started back from them with a striking appearance of horrour" (V.169). In another chapel, showing similar traces of this curious Hebridean custom of leaving exposed skeletons in churches, Boswell takes a spade and buries the bones he finds: "Dr. Johnson praised me for what I had done, though he owned, he could not have done it. . . . In the Charter-room there was a remarkably large shin-bone, which was said to have been a bone of *John Garve*, one of the lairds. Dr. Johnson would not look at it; but started away" (V.327).

Such moments are atypical. The journey, presenting a constant variety of new ideas, effectively silences that dialogue of the mind with itself which is at the heart of Johnson's suffering. The *Tour* represents an interlude in the life of the hero, and Boswell's most frequent effort is to capture the holiday atmosphere, with its overtones of psychological escape, through external description: "one night, in Col, he strutted about the room with a broad-sword and target, and made a formidable appearance; and, another night, I took the liberty to put a large blue bonnet on his head. His age, his size, and his bushy grey wig, with this covering on it, presented the image of a venerable *Senachi*" (V.324). In such scenes the sterner aspect of Johnson's public (London) personality dissolves in a mood of utter playfulness, and Boswell reminds us of it only to show the completeness of the transformation. As when, in one Highland house, a young lady puts her arms around Johnson's neck and kisses him: " 'do it again, (said he,) and let us see who will tire first.'—He kept her on his knee some time, while he and she drank tea. . . . To me it was highly comick, to see the grave philosopher,—the Rambler,—toying with a Highland beauty!" (V.261).

Such scenes, which again remind us of the comic romance theme of the *Tour*, reveal more than anything else the degree to which Johnson's Highland journey represents a psychological escape: this is a Johnson we shall never see in the *Life*. The mood of release carries over to the end of the *Tour*, where Johnson re-enters with a new attitude the familiar world he has for three months abandoned in search of wild and primitive nature and society. As they approach Edinburgh, Johnson's thoughts move from the romantic attractions of the western islands to the comforts of civilization, and he appears almost as an explorer emerging from the wilderness after a long journey: "as we walked up from the shore, Dr. Johnson's heart was cheered by the sight of a road marked with cartwheels, as on the main land; a thing which we had not seen for a long time. It gave us pleasure similar to that which a traveler feels, when, whilst wandering on what he fears is a desert island, he perceives the print of human feet" (V.322).

Johnson's emergence from the Hebrides represents an imaginative as well as a geographical transition, and Boswell, as usual, catches the psychological truth in an external posture. At the inn in Glasgow, says Boswell, "he enjoyed in imagination the comforts which we could now command, and seemed to be in high glee. I remember, he put a leg up on each side of the grate, and said, with a mock solemnity, by way of soliloquy, but loud enough for me to hear it, 'Here am I, an ENGLISH man, sitting by a *coal* fire' " (V.369). At the beginning of the *Tour* Johnson's acceptance of London life as normal reality lent the primitive and wild world of the Scottish Highlands its imaginative attraction. But life in the Hebrides has eventually taken on the aspect of the everyday, and at the end of the narrative it is London that has receded enough to become an idea. Johnson now approaches his normal sphere of existence with the same heightened enjoyment that someone just come in from a storm will appreciate a fire and a warm bed. This is the meaning of a passage which is sometimes quoted to show Johnson's antiprimitivism, but which in fact means something quite different: "we had a pleasing conviction of the commodiousness of civilization," reports Boswell when he and Johnson find themselves being carried along in a comfortable carriage, "and heartily laughed at the ravings of those absurd visionaries who have attempted to persuade us of the superior advantage of a *state of nature*" (V.365).

At Edinburgh, Johnson resumes the character of moralist and great man that he has to some extent abandoned in his role as traveler, and we find him once again at the center of the kind of scene we associate with the *Life:* literary conversation, wit, Johnson holding forth to a circle of attentive admirers, and so on. Boswell's house in Edinburgh becomes a version of Bolt-court or the Mitre tavern: "on the mornings when he breakfasted at my house, he had, from ten o'clock till one or two, a constant levée of various persons, of very different characters and descriptions. I could not attend him, being obliged to be in the Court of Sessions; but my wife was so good as to devote the greater part of the morning to the endless task of pouring out tea for my friend and his visitors" (V.395). We do not have any of the conversation that went on at these levees, only a kind of tableau of Johnson once again established in his London role, placed in the full light of universal respect and recognition.

The *Tour* closes with Johnson's departure for London, the great theater of life and animated exertion. But if London is the symbol, in Boswell's narrative, of animation and exertion, it is also associated with the painful personal struggle that is to become the main theme of the *Life of Johnson*. Now, after three months in the Hebrides, even London has for Johnson the attraction of a new place, or at least an old place seen in a new light, and his happy departure for the capital is the logical end of a tour that has freed Johnson for a time from what he once calls the pain of being a man. Boswell's view of his hero's "transit over the Caledonian hemisphere," for all its concentration on Johnson's external progress, its preoccupation with public posture and exclusion of psychological speculation, has caught the essential psychological truth.

FOUR

The public view of Johnson presented in the *Tour* is stylized and deliberately limited, representing the hero as seen by his society and age. Johnson the High Tory, the monarchist and Church of England man, author of *Rasselas* and the *Rambler* and "The Vanity of Human Wishes," is a figure who in his own lifetime has passed into the realm of public myth: "Dr. Samuel Johnson's character," we recall Boswell saying, "religious, moral, political and literary, nay his figure and manner are, I believe, more generally known than those of almost any man." The public view of Johnson appeals essentially to the enlarged and simplified notion of character that legends are made of, and in the *Tour* we see at work, on a level that at times moves close to caricature, a version of the evaluative process that is usually left to posterity.

At the same time, our impression of Johnson as hero of the *Tour* is larger and more complex than this public perspective allows for. Legends are always true, perhaps, in one sense—there is a kind of truth in our impulse to escape the sphere of unadorned reality—yet they can never contain the whole truth, for behind the legend there always lurks the figure of the private man, a creature of mixed motives and human inconsistencies. The tension that exists in life between man and legend becomes in Boswell a literary motif, a carefully balanced counterpoint between the public and private views of the hero. The commodiousness of Boswellian narrative, which allows the hero so much room for direct and personal expression, is part of its basic strategy, and Johnson in the *Tour*, as in the *Life*, ultimately contributes to our total impression of his personality an unmediated revelation of private concerns.

Johnson's behavior in the *Tour* works toward an impression of his state of mind that parallels Boswell's view of the journey as escape from self. Again one is apt to discover the idea of escape in the absence of those darker concerns that haunt the *Life*. There Johnson's constant horror of death becomes a major theme, the principal element in a personal struggle that is ultimately tragic. In the *Tour* the subject appears only in an occasional scene, and we glimpse the momentary recurrence of an inner conflict that has been otherwise suspended: "as I wandered with my revered friend in the groves of Auchinleck, I told him, that, if I survived him, it was my intention to erect a monument to him here, among scenes which, in my mind, were all classical. . . . He could not bear to have death presented to him in any shape; for his constitutional melancholy made the king of terrors more frightful. He turned off the subject, saying, 'Sir, I hope to see your grand-children!' " (V.380).

The single incident at Auchinleck is opposite in mood to the rest of the *Tour*, for the Highland journey has restored to Johnson a sense of youth and energy that for the moment postpones his usual terror of the inevitable. Against the Auchinleck episode we may set all those scenes which show Johnson in a state of high optimism: "yesterday Dr. Johnson said, 'I cannot but laugh, to think of myself roving among the Hebrides at sixty. I wonder where I shall rove at fourscore!' " (V.278). At other times the immediacy of death has so far receded that Johnson's usual anxiety is replaced by a calm and philosophical frame, as during his passage by sea to Mull: "Dr. Johnson, with compusure and solemnity, repeated the observation of Epictetus, that, 'as a man has the voyage of death before him,—whatever may be his employment, he should be ready at the master's call; and an old man should never be far from the shore, lest he should not be able to get himself ready' " (V.279).

In the Hebrides the introspective (and, to a degree, the speculative) side of Johnson's personality gives way to his role as active observer. His absorption in the role is reflected in his new concern with practical life, in the amount of his conversation that deals not with monarchy or Christianity, with salvation and grace and the powers of Parliament, but with the useful arts: "before dinner we examined the fort. . . . Dr. Johnson talked of the proportions of charcoal and salt-peter in making gunpowder, of granulating it, and of giving it a gloss. He made a very good figure upon these topics" (V.124); "I have often been astonished with what exactness he will explain the process of any art. He this morning explained to us all the operation of coining, and, at night, all the operation of brewing, so very clearly, that Mr. M'Queen said, when he heard the first, he thought he had been bred in the Mint; when he heard the second, that he had been bred a brewer" (V.215); "he talked both of threshing and thatching. . . . He said, a roof thatched with Lincolnshire reeds would last seventy years, as he was informed when in that country; and that he told this in London to a great thatcher, who said, he believed it might be true" (V.263).

Eventually, Johnson's apparently inexhaustible knowledge of the practical arts leads Boswell to try an experiment. "Last night," says Boswell, "Dr. Johnson gave us an account of the whole process of tanning,—and of the nature of milk, and the various operations upon it, as making whey, &c. . . . A strange thought struck me, to try if he knew anything of an art, or whatever it should be called, which is no doubt very useful in life, but which lies far out of the way of a philosopher and poet; I mean the trade of a butcher." Boswell begins the conversation with a discussion of the arts known to savage nations and attempts to steer Johnson toward the topic; after a few tries he succeeds: "by degrees, he shewed that he knew something even of butchery. 'Different animals (said he) are killed differently. An ox is knocked down, and a calf stunned, but a sheep has its throat cut" (V.246–47). And so on, until we have the full views of the philosopher and poet on butchery.

We shall seldom see this side of Johnson in the *Life*. Except when Henry Thrale dies, leaving Johnson as one of his executors, and we see Johnson bustling about with a pen and inkhorn and general air of importance, taking inventory and enjoying his role as a man of affairs, there are few parallels in the *Life* to these Hebridean conversations about the problems and arts of practical life. But we feel that Johnson's struggle in the *Life* has in some degree arisen from his *not* having just such an active role, the sense of structure and steady occupation that keeps the mind from preying on itself and relieves a man, whether he thinks about it or not, from the more morbid aspects of a life where all sense of purpose must come from within. In the *Tour* Johnson's only steady occupation is as a traveler, but in practical inquiry he finds a release from gloomy introspection and in practical conversation an affirmation of his role as active observer.

In the Hebrides, too, we see Johnson indulging a romantic nationalism clearly associated with his role as traveler. Among foreign scenes, perhaps, every traveler feels a strangeness that the mind attempts to accommodate by idealizing the familiar, but Johnson's idealization of the English character in the *Tour* is also an effect of distance. Viewed from afar, away from disputed national issues and the venality of party politics, England becomes an idea to which the imagination can respond uncritically. In one mood, Johnson's exaltation of the English takes the form of robust, half-jocular assertions of national superiority: "*Boswell*. 'You yourself, sir, have never seen, till now, any thing but your native island.'—*Johnson*. 'But, sir, by seeing London, I have seen as much of life as the world can shew.'—*Boswell*. 'You have

not seen Pekin.'—*Johnson.* 'What is Pekin? Ten thousand Lon-
doners would *drive* all the people of Pekin: they would drive
them like deer' " (V.305). In another, it is based in something
very close to nostalgia; as when, while breakfasting one morning,
Johnson and Boswell turn to talking of Goldsmith's *Traveller:*
"while I was helping him on with his great coat, he repeated from
it the character of the British nation, which he did with such
energy, that the tear started into his eye:

> Stern o'er each bosom reason holds her state,
> With daring aims irregularly great,
> Pride in their port, defiance in their eye,
> I see the lords of humankind pass by. . . ." (V.345)

Johnson's romantic nationalism in the *Tour,* like Goldsmith's
poem, exalts English independence and liberty and takes as an
implicit background all the historical scenes, from the signing of
the Magna Carta onward, that are traditionally associated with
the folklore of national liberty. English liberty, of course, has
produced that sturdy race of yeomen who are the glory of the
nation, brave in battle, independent in thought, and vigorous to
a degree impossible in countries denied the twin blessings of roast
beef and the British constitution. The same notion lies behind
Johnson's numerous comparisons of the English and the French.
If the Highland journey were to raise in Johnson's mind any idea
of national contrast, one might suppose it would be that between
England and Scotland. But Johnson's gibes at the Scotch, though
they recur throughout the *Tour,* follow essentially the same tone
as those we find scattered throughout the *Life,* and they are always qualified by Johnson's unfailing politeness to his Scottish
hosts and admirers. Johnson's distance from home has evoked a
mood in which the Scotch are unsuitable adversaries, and he turns
most often to the conventional eighteenth-century comparison,
based in competing national interests, which had been a staple of
patriotic English oratory since Shakespeare's day.

Johnson's remarks on the English and the French are almost a separate motif of his conversation in the *Tour*. We learn, unsurprisingly enough, that Englishmen are bigger, stronger, more vigorous, and above all more intellectually independent than the servile subjects of an absolute monarch: " 'it is thought by sensible military men, that the English do not enough avail themselves of their superior strength of body against the French; for that must always have a great advantage in pushing with bayonets. . . . the weaker-bodied French must be overcome by our strong soldiers' " (V.229–30); " 'the English (said he) are the only nation who ride hard a-hunting. A Frenchman goes out upon a managed horse, and capers in the field, and no more thinks of leaping a hedge than of mounting a breach' " (V.253); "Dr. Johnson observed, that there was nothing of which he would not undertake to persuade a Frenchman in a foreign country. 'I'll carry a Frenchman to St. Paul's Church-yard, and I'll tell him, "by our law you may walk half round the church; but, if you walk round the whole, you will be punished capitally:" and he will believe me at once. Now, no Englishman would readily swallow such a thing: he would go and inquire of somebody else' " (V.330).

Johnson in his role as traveler, as active observer, as uncritical nationalist, is Johnson in a strangely peaceful and even complacent frame of mind. Our ultimate assurance of this is the absence in the *Tour* of those tokens of personal suffering that will so strongly inform the portrait of Johnson in the *Life*. In the Hebrides, Johnson can even talk about his melancholy in the most detached terms, a sure indication that he is not suffering at the moment: " 'I inherited, (said he,) a vile melancholy from my father, which has made me mad all my life, at least not sober.'—Lady M'Leod wondered he should tell this" (V.215). In the *Life* Boswell will write to Johnson again and again to complain of his own suffering, and Johnson's answers always represent variations on a single theme: "you are always complaining of melancholy, and I conclude from those complaints that you are

landed at Tobermorie, 'We shall see Dr. M'Lean, who has written the history of the M'Leans.'—*Johnson*. 'I have not great patience to stay and hear the history of the M'Leans. I would rather hear the History of the Thrales' " (V.313). But Johnson's fretfulness always disappears when his attention is again taken up by outward scenes, and we see his vicissitude of mind only as a tendency.

Johnson in the *Tour* is otherwise completely good humored, viewing his own existence and the world complacently. One index of this mood is the frequency with which he is moved to nostalgia and reminiscence. In the *Life* Johnson will often regard his earlier years with a sense of pain, and on those rare occasions when his mind is enough at rest to do otherwise, his reminiscence will take place offstage. "This evening," Boswell will say, "Dr. Johnson was kind enough to give me many particulars of his early life," and we will be referred to the account of Johnson's youth which takes up the first part of the biography. But Johnson in the *Tour* often takes the same detached view of his early life as of death and melancholy, and in doing so reveals a changed attitude toward himself and his existence: "*Johnson*. 'Why, sir, a man grows better humoured as he grows older. He improves by experience. When young, he thinks himself of great consequence, and every thing of importance. As he advances in life, he learns to think himself of no consequence, and little things of little importance; and so he becomes more patient, and better pleased' " (V.211). Johnson's reference to his own case is implicit. In the *Life* Johnson will repudiate any suggestion that old age has its advantages with a scorn that barely conceals his anxiety (one thinks of the meeting with his cheerful schoolfellow, Edwards). But when the mind is at ease one discovers the positive aspects even of old age.

So as Johnson moves through the Hebrides we often see his thoughts turning to his earlier years, to his days of obscurity in London and even to his youth in Lichfield: "he said, that, 'when he lodged in the Temple, and had no regular system of life, he had fasted for two days at a time, during which he had gone about visiting, though not at the hours of dinner or supper; that he had drunk tea, but eaten no bread; that this was no intentional fasting, but happened just in the course of a literary life' " (V.284); "in the last age, when my mother lived in London, there were two sets of people, those who gave the wall, and those who took it; the peaceable and the quarrelsome. When I returned to Lichfield, after having been in London, my mother asked me, whether I was one of those who gave the wall, or those who took it" (V.230). Such spontaneous recollections of the past are significant just because of the part we expect them to play in an older man's conversation; in the *Tour*, with his fear of old age for the moment suspended, Johnson can for the time enjoy reminiscence, looking back on his past life with pleasure.

Johnson's escape from melancholy appears, too, in all those scenes in the *Tour* where he indulges in joyous flights of pure fancy. These moments provide an ongoing motif, a continuous reminder that Johnson has for the time been released from that state of melancholy in which the mind preys upon itself and a man most feels the pain of being a man. When the travelers reach Saint Andrews, Boswell initiates one such imaginative flight: " 'if, (said I) our club should come and set up in St. Andrews, as a college, to teach all that each of us can, in the several departments of learning and taste, we should rebuild the city: we should draw a wonderful concourse of students.'—Dr. Johnson entered fully into the spirit of this project. We immediately fell to distributing the offices. I was to teach Civil and Scotch law; Burke, politicks and eloquence; Garrick, the art of publick speaking" (V.108). And so it goes, for a long paragraph, until all the professorships have been awarded.

Anyone who has read much Boswell will have come to expect this sort of thing from him, and the imaginary university does in fact have the Boswellian stamp of luxurious fantasy. But when we find Johnson joining in so readily, this imaginative play begins to determine the mood of the *Tour* as a whole, for it tells us much about the hero's present state of mind. And Johnson does not always depend on Boswell to begin the game. At Inch Keith we again see him playing with the idea of moving to a strange locale—"he said, 'I'd have this island. I'd build a house, make a good landing-place, have a garden, and vines, and all sorts of trees' " (V.56). M'Leod's offer to install Johnson on "a beautiful little island in the Loch of Dunvegan, called *Isa*" sets off another imaginative flight: "Dr. Johnson was highly amused with the fancy. I have seen him please himself with little things, even with mere ideas like the present. He talked a great deal of this island;—how he would build a house there,—how he would fortify it,—how he would have cannon,—how he would plant,—how he would sally out, and *take* the island of Muck;—and then he laughed with uncommon glee, and could hardly leave off" (V. 249).

Often in the *Life* we see Johnson laughing uproariously, but it is always when he has scored a particularly effective point in a dispute or when he has surprised even himself with a sudden turn of wit. But here, in an open boat threading its way among the Hebrides, it is a pure delight in extravagant fancy that moves Johnson to uncommon glee. Amidst the succession of new scenes offered by the journey, Johnson's mind is not only crowded with new images but enough at ease to work them into shapes pleasing to the imagination, a sure indication of just how completely melancholy has been banished for the time at hand. The Hebrides, the pastoral atmosphere, the traveler's preoccupation with what he sees have all combined to reinforce Johnson's sense that he has escaped that continuous struggle with himself that gives the darker portrait of the *Life* its tragic overtones.

Johnson's flights of fancy do not all center on the occasional island he can imagine as a Johnsonian domain, but crop up unexpectedly in the normal course of his conversation in the *Tour*.

When debating the merits of the Scottish claymore as a weapon, for instance, he does not weigh the problem in abstract terms but explains in graphic detail how he would fight a man armed with it (V.229). And a conversation about the advantages of wearing linen brings out a fantasy that we, along with Boswell, are likely to find highly comic: " 'I have often thought, that, if I kept a seraglio, the ladies should all wear linen gowns,—or cotton;—I mean stuffs made of vegetable substances. I would have no silk; you cannot tell when it is clean. . . .' To hear the grave Dr. Samuel Johnson, 'that majestick teacher of moral and religious wisdom,' while sitting solemn in an arm-chair in the isle of Sky, talk, *ex cathedra*, of his keeping a seraglio, and acknowledge that the sup-position had *often* been in his thoughts, struck me so forcibly with ludicrous contrast, that I could not but laugh immoderately" (V.216).

Yet this inadvertent glimpse of Johnson's personal fantasy-life fits the mood of the narrative very well. In the *Tour*, where we see Johnson strutting about the room in Highland dress, bouncing a young lady on his knee, or calmly quoting Epictetus on death, we come to expect that revelation of personality that occurs only when the hero is at his ease. For Johnson, who has passed his sixty-fifth birthday in the Hebrides, the journey has been both an adventure and a journey back into something very like youth, and the wild landscape of the western islands, with its associa-tions with the remote and heroic past and its present state of primitive simplicity, has provided the perfect setting. For John-son's spiritual struggle, with himself and the moral and intellec-tual forces that surround him, epitomizes the larger struggle of his time, an age of complicated strife where reason and faith have become enemies rather than allies. In such a context a journey to the Hebrides appears finally as a movement backward into time and simplicity, and a spiritual escape from larger conflict.

Though the *Tour* is about Johnson's travels in the Hebrides, we are never allowed to forget that (in Johnson's phrase) a man's journey is not only to something but away from something. "That man is never happy for the present is so true," says Johnson in the *Life*, "that all his relief from unhappiness is only forgetting himself for a little while": the words might be taken as an epigraph for the *Tour to the Hebrides*. Yet the very meaning of Johnson's journey as an escape from self depends on his not being like other men. If the *Tour* gives us the picture of a hero who has been able to forget himself for a little while, it contains too, in changed form, the elements of the great moral struggle that has made him a hero. In the *Life* the spiritual dilemma of the great man caught in an age of invisible strife, where the mind itself becomes the arena of battle, becomes the postulate upon which Boswell bases his idea of Johnson as hero, towering as much above his age as Caesar and Alexander did above theirs. Johnson as traveler is still *that* Johnson, and we have only a sense of fulfilled decorum when Boswell closes the *Tour* by calling it a book about "one whose virtues will, I hope, ever be an object of imitation, and whose powers of mind were so extraordinary, that ages may revolve before such a man shall again appear." (V.416).

3

A GREEN-GOOSE
AND A HERO

BOSWELL AS
BIOGRAPHICAL NARRATOR

IN THE CONTEXT of modern criticism as a whole, a suggestion that one approach a biographical work like the *Life of Johnson* as a self-contained world of motive and action is very nearly orthodox: literary critics are after all no longer much interested in discussing such questions as whether Shakespeare adequately represented the "real"—that is, the historical—Macbeth. Yet the strategic maneuver that carried literary theory around and past the strongly held position occupied by "factual" narrative also isolated modern readers with a serious interest in biography. It is easy enough to maintain, from a purely theoretical viewpoint, that the problem of biography will not be resolved until scholars and critics have learned to recognize as meaningful a mode of argument about the *Life of Johnson* making no reference to any "real" Boswell, any "real" Johnson, but a question remains about the direction in which this leads us.

If one looks backward, as it were, the path seems somehow comfortless: a solid world of presumed actuality recedes, and one is left with the *Life of Johnson* and two other biographical narratives written by James Boswell. The theorist's assurance that the *Life* and the *Tour to the Hebrides* represent worlds in themselves seems to offer little enough comfort at such a moment, and one may recover a sense of the dismay that once greeted the concept of autonomy as applied to the genres of imaginative literature. At the same time, one is reminded of how that general dismay eventually gave way before the discovery that literature may be meaningfully viewed as an autonomous realm, that interpretation at the level of relations among works may approach a poem or play or novel as belonging, if not to the world of everyday reality, to the universe of literature perceived as a simultaneous order. Here perhaps is the comfort one seeks: if we have left behind a situation where comparison of Boswellian narrative with "objective" reality tells us little, we have entered a realm where comparison with the *Odyssey* or eighteenth-century comedy may tell us everything.

Seen in this light, biography in general and Boswellian narrative in particular appear in a new focus, and one becomes aware not only of new problems in literary and symbolic meaning that need to be solved but of possible solutions to old problems. In this latter category we may place the problem, something of a crux in Boswell scholarship, of Boswell as biographical narrator. It is significant not only that the question of Boswell's role as narrator of his own works is problematic precisely as the status of biography has remained problematic—indeed one reads in its successive formulations the history of Boswell criticism writ small—but that its resolution along the lines followed in this essay requires that we approach biography, and not simply Boswell's contributions to the genre, in a new way.

In the nineteenth century the problem was not perceived as a problem: Boswell as he appeared in his works *was* Boswell, and any suggestion that one inquire into the "meaning" of his role as narrator would have met with polite incredulity. In this context Macaulay's picture of Boswell as an inspired idiot who managed to write a great work precisely because of his assiduous sychophancy could be taken as conclusive. In less vitriolic form the same response can be found among Boswell's contemporaries.

We may take as our text Thomas Gray's comment, well known
to Boswellians, on the *Tour to Corsica:* "Mr. Boswell's book . . .
has pleased and moved me strangely, all (I mean) that relates to
Paoli. He is a man born two thousand years after his time! The
pamphlet proves what I have always maintained, that any fool
may write a most valuable book by chance, if he will only tell us
what he saw and heard with veracity. Of Mr. Boswell's truth I
have not the least suspicion, because I am sure he could invent
nothing of this kind. The true title of this part of his work is, 'A
Dialogue Between a Green-goose and a Hero.' "[1]

Even when we suspend questions about any "real" Boswell,
we may see that certain elements of Gray's description remain
surprisingly suggestive, especially his awareness that Boswell's
narrative is simultaneously concerned with an impression of complete veracity and with the hero as a figure existing spiritually
outside his own age. At the same time, any suspension of the
usual questions leads, as we have observed, to a search for the
internal or symbolic principles controlling biography as a literary
form. This is the context, long since explored elsewhere in modern criticism, in which a concern with one or two or three works
moves irresistibly toward a perception of literature as composing
a simultaneous order.

The problem of Boswell's role as narrator is in this sense a
problem in literary conventions, if by conventions we mean the
symbolic principles governing literary forms. The nature of the
problem thus directs us to consider not the role of the narrator
in biography merely, but of a narrator always seen in relation to
some biographical hero, for only within the symbolic dimensions
of this essential relationship do we discover the conventions that
allow us meaningfully to discuss biography as a narrative mode.
The dim beginnings of this mode, as Arnaldo Momigliano has
pointed out in *The Development of Greek Biography*, are to be
found in the *bios* of the hero, a form of "mythical biography"
which concerned the lives of such heroes as Heracles, Theseus,

and Oedipus.[2] No example of these *bioi* exists today—Momigliano is working by careful and delicate inference from fragmentary materials—but the form adduced suggests much about the conventions of later biographical narrative.

If we concentrate for the moment on the figure of the hero, we may perceive in the *bios* form (I use this as shorthand for "*bios* of the hero") a symbolic paradigm that was to serve as well for the medieval saint or the great man of the eighteenth and nineteenth centuries as for Heracles or Theseus, and which answers a number of troublesome questions about biographies we are accustomed to regard as classics. For the mode of mythical biography described by Momigliano would in one crucial aspect have resembled epic, positing the existence of an unseen world behind the visible one and giving us the hero as Victor Brombert describes him: "god, demigod, or intimate with the gods, he provided a transcendental link between the contingencies of the finite and the imagined realm of the supernatural. Time and the timeless, man's mortal state and the realm of eternal laws, were brought through him into conflict with each other. Through him also these orders overlapped."[3]

The hero in this situation is a symbolic figure in part because most men, including the narrator and readers of his story, are not heroes—as ordinary beings, they look as it were through the hero to an unseen world whose existence is normally a matter of faith or belief. Though this does not in itself explain the symbolic structure of all biographies, it is at least evident that something like the *bios* principle is at work in widely varying forms of biographical literature. This is why, for instance, when Plato and Xenophon tell us about the daimon of Socrates, we are no longer dealing with Socrates merely as a philosopher but as a philosopher-hero divinely possessed. For similar reasons Plutarch's description of the supernatural happenings following Caesar's death—"the great comet, which shone very bright for seven nights after Caesar's death, and then disappeared, and the dimness of the sun, which remained pale and dull for the whole of that year"—unavoidably reminds us of the events surrounding Christ's death in the Gospels, and both dramatize the hero's participation in an unseen world.

Ancient biography, written in an age when the gods still spoke through oracles, drew unselfconsciously on the elaborate mythologies that survive in Homer and Virgil. In the Christian era we discover an obvious version of the *bios* form in the medieval saint's life, where the unseen world always appears as a providential presence interfering miraculously on behalf of the religious hero or heroine. After the Renaissance, as the idea of an unseen external order gradually gave way to an inner order of subjective and intense experience inaccessible to ordinary men, the hero of the *bios* form became the hero as Carlyle described him in the nineteenth century, one "who lives in the inward sphere of things, in the True, Divine, and Eternal." Thus Southey's Nelson, standing on his deck in a moment of "prophetic glory"—"from that time, he often said, a radiant orb was suspended in his mind's eye, which urged him onward to renown"— is as much in contact with an unseen world as Theseus or Heracles, and thus Norman Malcolm's recent *Memoir* of Wittgenstein is able to portray a philosopher-hero as much possessed by a daimon as Socrates.

When we search for symbolic continuities in the tradition of English biography to which Boswellian narrative belongs, we may trace the beginnings of the long transition from medieval to modern back to Roper's *Life of More*, a sixteenth-century narrative which, even as it portrays More as a complex figure living uneasily in a Machiavellian world of power and intrigue, possesses strong affinities with the saint's life. In the seventeenth century, amid a growing stream of biographical writing, Walton's *Lives* looks back over two centuries to both the *bios* form and the hagiographic tradition. Both Roper and Walton, unable to portray their heroes as figures participating directly in an unseen order, shift their emphasis to the almost supernatural piety of the hero, yet strong evidences of the miraculous remain, giving us in Roper such scenes as that in which More's prayers rescue his dying daughter—"God showed, as it seemed, a manifest miraculous token of his special favor towards him"—and in Walton such episodes as Donne's mysterious vision of his absent wife and daughter.

At the same time, the symbolic relation of the hero to an unseen or divine world had become problematic for biographers in the *bios* tradition. Writing at the dawn of the age of the Royal Society, Walton is compelled to undertake an anxious defense of his own credibility, as when he addresses his audience after giving an account of Donne's miraculous vision: "if the unbelieving will not allow the believing reader of this story a liberty to believe that it may be true, then I wish him to consider, many wise men have believed that the ghost of Julius Caesar did appear to Brutus, and that both St. Austin, and Monica his mother, had visions in order to his conversion." As Walton's anxieties suggest, the *bios* in its traditional form was becoming untenable in a climate of thought soon to come under the influence of Newton's *Principia* and Locke's *Essay on Human Understanding*, for a narrator can scarcely look beyond his hero to an unseen world when the unseen world, at least as a miraculous or mysterious presence, has ceased to exist.

By the time Boswell began writing biographical narrative a century later, in an age increasingly troubled by the powerful scepticism of the Enlightenment, only some compromise with the phenomenon of unbelief would leave the biographer free to continue working in the *bios* tradition. As we have seen, Boswell was not only to achieve this compromise but to discover within its context a new kind of biographical hero, a figure standing in solitary opposition to the Enlightenment as represented by such philosophes as Hume and Voltaire and Holbach, an age of moral chaos and revolutionary tendencies in which men, to borrow

Burke's phrase once again, had shrunk from their natural dimensions. To fully understand the nature of Boswell's compromise,
however, one must turn from the role of the hero in the *bios* form
to the role of the narrator, and to what might be called the symbolic dimension of the relationship between them.

The narrator and hero of the *bios* tradition are coordinate figures, for as the hero is an extraordinary being participating in a
world invisible to ordinary men, the narrator is a spokesman for
the ordinary world, and his role is symbolic in a sense well described by Thomas Edwards: the ordinary man, Edwards points
out, "is, like 'the hero,' a fiction. . . . The normal has meaning only
in reference to the abnormal, the unexpected phenomenon that
creates an opposing sense of mutuality where none was apparent
before."[4] In its simplest form the coordinate relation of narrator
and hero demands only the implied notion of ordinariness we
find in ancient biography—where the narrator, as in Plutarch or
Nepos, exists outside the story he is telling—or in the medieval
saint's life—where the hero is identified with a divine world of
grace and miracles and the narrator with unredeemed mankind.

In English biography we may again turn to Roper's *Life of
More* and Walton's *Lives* as reflecting changes in the *bios* form
in the two centuries before Boswell. As biographical narrators
both Roper and Walton bear a strong resemblance to the anonymous storytellers of the saints' lives, though in the more personal
context of their narratives the narrator's identification with unredeemed mankind is replaced by a sense of unworthiness in relation to their heroes, as when Roper represents himself as "most
unworthy" to tell More's story, Walton as "the poorest, the
meanest" of Donne's friends. At the same time, the Renaissance
saw an important change in the *bios* form, for in Roper we have
for the first time in English biography a narrator who has eaten
and talked and joked with the hero, and in Roper's recollections
of his conversations with More—"so on a time walking with me
along the Thames side at Chelsea, in talking of other things he said

unto me"—we discover the beginnings of an altered biographical tradition leading to the *Life of Johnson*.

Once more we are dealing with the symbolic dimensions of the narrator-hero relationship central to the *bios* form, and now with the narrator as placed in a new and vulnerable situation. For when intimacy with the hero is introduced as a narrative principle in biography, both narrator and hero exist within the confines of a single dramatic situation, and the moral superiority separating the hero from ordinary mankind appears specifically as superiority to the narrator. The great danger, of course, is that the symbolic or representative dimension of his "ordinariness" will simply collapse, and that he will emerge as a prosaic and credulous speaker whose estimate of the hero's greatness fails to win our assent. The way in which Roper and Walton moved to circumvent this danger returns us to the problem of veracity raised in Gray's comments on the *Tour to Corsica*.

In one important sense we may say that Roper, Walton, and Boswell reached nearly identical solutions to the problem of veracity, the illusion of purely factual truth that among other things defines biography as a narrative genre. An awareness of the problem moves Roper in the *Life of More* to assume a posture where a certain artlessness or naiveté becomes a guarantee of fidelity, as is evident even in the way he speaks of his role as narrator of More's story: "I have as far forth as my mean wit, memory, and knowledge would serve me, declared so much thereof as in my poor judgement seemed worthy to be remembered." A century later we encounter Walton's "artless pencil, guided by the hand of truth"—this same artlessness, he assures us, "ought to beget faith in what is spoken: for he that wants skill to deceive may safely be trusted"—and a motif of conscious naiveté which runs throughout the *Lives*.

Our search for symbolic continuities in the *bios* tradition brings us not only to the emergence of the naive narrator in such works as the *Life of More* and Walton's *Lives*, but to a point where we may perceive the odd suggestiveness of one of Gray's comments on the *Tour to Corsica:* "of Mr. Boswell's truth I have not the least suspicion, because I am sure he could invent nothing of this kind." In Boswell's version of the *bios* the naiveté of the storyteller operates as in Roper and Walton as a guarantee of truthfulness; but something essential, moral sympathy for the narrator in relation to the hero, has clearly been lost. The compromise through which Boswell won the freedom to work within the *bios* tradition thus underlies the central paradox of Boswell's biographical narratives—that they reveal Pascal Paoli and Samuel Johnson as genuine moral heroes even as Boswell, in his veneration of them, seems somehow foolish and excessive.

A consideration of the *bios* tradition in English biography allows us not only to isolate this paradox in its formal or conventional aspect but to explain its meaning through examination of the symbolic structure of Boswellian narrative. To this we may now turn, with one final observation on the evolution of the *bios* form: though Roper and Walton discovered in the naive or artless narrator an important solution to a difficult formal problem, they did so while remaining within the comparatively safe bounds of the hagiographic tradition, and managed to write a kind of biography still sustained by a notion of the hero's participation in a divine and coherent order. As the artlessness of a biographical narrator appears in this context as an aspect of his unworthiness, and as this unworthiness merely identifies him with unredeemed mankind, his naiveté and simplicity appear as attractive and even virtuous qualities. In the secular, low mimetic world of Boswellian narrative no such universal standard of human unworthiness exists, and naiveté is seen not as virtuous simplicity but as naiveté.

There is a certain poignancy in Boswell's attempts to draw attention, during his own lifetime, to what we should call the modern distinction between author and narrator, as when in the dedication to the *Life of Johnson* he writes in defense of certain scenes in the earlier *Tour to the Hebrides* which had shown him

among the victims of Johnson's wit: "I trusted I should be liber-
ally understood, as knowing very well what I was about, and by
no means as simply unconscious of the pointed effects of the satire. I own, indeed, that I was arrogant enough to suppose that
the tenour of the rest of the book would sufficiently guard me
against such a strange imputation." Boswell's protests, over-
whelmed by the powerful illusion of actuality we have seen to be
associated with the naive narrator of the *bios* tradition, were to
have little effect: for Macaulay, describing Boswell as an inspired
idiot who had managed to write a great book, and for Gray, describing one Boswellian narrative as a dialogue between a green-
goose and a hero, the naive narrator and the biographer were
indistinguishable figures.

As they concern the symbolic structure of Boswellian narrative, however, such remarks serve to locate Boswell as a biographical narrator in the formal tradition of the naïf or ingénu
and as belonging to a literary family extending back through
Chaucer in the *Canterbury Tales* and Dante in the *Commedia* to
ancient literature. It is from this perspective, for instance, that
we hear John Lockhart, the great nineteenth-century biographer
of Walter Scott, describing Boswell's role as narrator in terms
that remind us of a modern critic discussing Lemuel Gulliver:
"never did any man tell a story with such liveliness and fidelity,
and yet contrive to leave so strong an impression that he did not
himself understand it . . . unconscious all the while, of the real
gist and bearing of the facts he is relating."[5] Only Lockhart's
assumptions about biography, which are roughly the assumptions
of Gray and Macaulay, convert so promising an insight into a
matter of perplexity.

At the same time, one may discover traces of these same assumptions in modern Boswell criticism, and along with them an
underlying tension in discussions of Boswell's role as narrator.
It is today a commonplace of Boswell criticism, for instance, to
describe Boswell as an Everyman figure and to discover in the

description a double significance. When undertaken in the interests of literary interpretation, as in Paul Alkon's fine essay on
aesthetic distance in the *Life of Johnson*[6] or in Frank Brady's
enlightening discussion of Boswell's manner of self-presentation,[7]
the description normally refers to some aspect of what we have
called the symbolic "ordinariness" of the narrator in the *bios*
tradition. More often, however, the description is merely honor-
ific, a twentieth-century reaction against Macaulay operating on
nineteenth-century assumptions, where to see Boswell as Everyman is to see him as someone very much like the rest of us and
not (unless we are all idiots) as the inspired idiot Macaulay
described.

An inquiry into the meaning of Boswell's role as narrator will
lead away from this kind of reasoning and toward a fuller consideration of the relationship between narrator and hero in Boswell's three major biographical narratives. Here, as with the
figure of the naive narrator, Boswell found freedom through
compromise: writing in an age when the hero's participation in
an unseen world was no longer credible, and when the notion of a
heroic inner world of subjective experience had not altogether
emerged, Boswell managed to create a version of the *bios* form
by portraying his heroes as figures living outside their time, existing within a private order of the moral imagination looking
back to an idea of spiritual coherence associated with an earlier
age. Once again we encounter the subject of Boswellian narrative
as the hero in an unheroic world, with such men as Paoli and
Samuel Johnson appearing in it as isolated beings in a time that,
in Carlyle's phrase, denies the desirableness of great men.

When we consider the symbolic structure of Boswell's narratives, then, we are dealing not only with the relation of the
narrator as naïf to the figure of the isolated hero but with the
phenomenon of scepticism or unbelief as possessing a double
significance in the opposing worlds of narrator and hero. In portraying Paoli and Johnson as figures existing out of their time,

Boswell creates around his heroes a private world of the moral imagination in which the rational scepticism we associate with the Enlightenment, the noble and emancipating weapon of the philosophes, is seen in the dark and pessimistic light in which Carlyle described it—"not intellectual doubt alone, but moral doubt; all sorts of infidelity, insincerity, spiritual paralysis." This is, as Carlyle saw, the spiritual paralysis of an age which among other things denies the very possibility of heroism.

In Paoli's identification with the heroes of antiquity, or in Johnson's Toryism and orthodoxy and monarchical principles, we have a notion of the past as spiritual refuge and a concept of the hero as an isolated figure surrounded by invisible forces of moral anarchy. This is why the eighteenth century as portrayed in Boswell's narratives appears always in a double perspective. As a world of ordinary men with ordinary concerns, it is the busy, optimistic, confident world of the philosophes, the secular, low mimetic realm of Fielding or Smollett or the comic scenes in the *Life of Johnson*. Within the larger circumference of this world, however, exists the separate world of Boswell's heroes, and it is as we gaze through one to the other that we perceive the age in its darker aspect, as a time when "old opinions, feelings—ancestral customs and institutions are crumbling away, and both the spiritual and temporal worlds are darkened by the shadow of change."

Yet Boswell as a narrator in the *bios* tradition belongs not to the separate spiritual and imaginative world of his heroes but to the ordinary world beyond its perimeters—the eighteenth century of London shopkeepers, country squires, pamphleteers, free thinkers and philosophes. In this symbolic situation lies the meaning of what we have called the paradox of Boswellian narrative, for as a narrator representing ordinary mankind Boswell appears in his own works as a creature of the world he portrays, a speaker wholly subject—as his heroes are not—to the norms of his society and age. In this world, which is the world of Enlightenment rationalism, scepticism is the ironic detachment of Hume or Gibbon or Voltaire, an intellectual attitude that smiles at veneration and mocks enthusiasm, and makes a naïf of the biographer whose temper does not answer to its own.

If we see Paoli and Johnson as heroes living in an unheroic world, maintaining their private visions of coherence in an age of spiritual crisis, we see Boswell as a narrator whose preoccupation with great men is part of his own struggle to discover faith and order amid the moral disarray of the later eighteenth century. This is the final meaning of Boswell's naiveté, for when belief in a transcendent order is universal, men fall down before Poseidon or worship Christ as a matter of course, and excesses of awe or veneration are not excesses. When coherence has disappeared, we have the detached scepticism of Hume or Gibbon or, in biography, of Strachey. But in a period of transition—the eighteenth century as portrayed by Boswell or Burke, the nineteenth as seen by Arnold or Yeats—the Everyman narrator of the *bios* form is himself an odd and inconsistent figure, a naïf as out of place in the modern age as his heroes are, but on the ordinary or comic level, and unable to sacrifice his veneration of great men to a bleak ethic of ironic detachment.

TWO

The *Tour to Corsica*, which is sometimes described as Plutarchan, actually belongs in the *bios* category, for as it concerns Boswell the *Tour* is the story of an impressionable young man suddenly confronted with a hero who "lives in the inward sphere of things," and gives us our earliest example of the Boswellian narrator, a speaker who looks through the hero not to an unseen world but to the possibility of an order of coherence unperceived by ordinary men. This is a symbolic situation retaining a strong element of mystery, and in *Corsica* even a suggestion of

the miraculous. We are not surprised, for instance, to learn that
Paoli sometimes has prophetic visions, though Boswell is sufficiently uneasy about relating the fact, "knowing how much it
may be ridiculed in an age when mankind are so fond of incredulity that they seem to pique themselves in contracting their
circle of belief as much as possible" (194). Paoli appears in *Corsica* as a hero in the Plutarchan mold, but this is only because
Boswell's "naive" perception of the world provides an expanded
circle of belief impervious to rational scepticism.

In one respect, therefore, *Corsica* participates in the general
conflict of imagination and reason we have in mind when we call
the later eighteenth century an age of sensibility. But only in a
limited way, for the imaginative impulse that produced the Goth-
ic novel or the Ossian poems was fundamentally self-conscious
and represented a cultivation of the mysterious or the primitive
or the sublime for its own sake. The element of mystery involved
in Boswell's vision of Paoli as a Plutarchan hero, on the other
hand, like the romantic primitivism involved in his idea of the
Corsicans as inhabitants of the Golden Age, derives not from a
self-conscious attempt to explore areas of experience that lie beyond reason and scepticism but from a personal and spontaneous
urge to discover, through the imagination, a level of reality which
transcends the merely rational. This is an imaginative process
that begins in an instinctive attempt to establish a satisfactory
relationship between the self and the world.

As we have seen, Paoli's character as hero depends on a more
sustained version of this same process, for his imaginative identification with the heroes of ancient Greece and Rome is a means
of accommodating his own heroic aspirations to the unheroic
world of eighteenth-century Corsica. The Paoli who "just lives
in the times of antiquity" exists as it were inside an illusion, but
an illusion so magnanimous and complete that it becomes an alternative vision of reality. For Boswell, however, operating on an
average or ordinary level of human experience, the process in-

volves the more temporary sort of illusion we call fantasy. Early
in the narrative, for instance, the patriotism of some Corsican
peasants moves Boswell to sing them the English patriotic song
"Heart of Oak." The Corsicans are delighted, and their enthusiasm prompts a characteristic flight of imagination: " 'cuore di
quercia,' cried they, 'bravo Inglese!' It was quite a joyous riot. I
fancied myself to be a recruiting officer. I fancied all my chorus
of Corsicans aboard the British fleet" (185–86).

Such moments recur throughout the *Tour to Corsica* and are
really examples of overheard fantasy or momentary triumphs of
the imagination over literal experience. The degree of self-
revelation involved once again emphasizes Boswell's character as
naïf, for we overhear his fantasies only because he is innocent
enough to record them, apparently unaware that the same process
that puts Paoli and the Corsicans in a heroic light reveals him as innocent and somewhat credulous. As Boswell comes to see Corsica
more and more as an island existing in happy isolation from the
modern age and preserving the simple virtues of heroic antiquity, the impulse to identify becomes so strong that he will occasionally assume an imaginary character and step into the scene
he is describing. This happens, for instance, when the appearance
of some Corsican fighters inspires Boswell to take the part of a
Roman orator or a general addressing his troops: "I harangued
the men of Bastelica with great fluency. I expiated on the bravery
of the Corsicans by which they had purchased liberty . . . and
rendered themselves glorious over all Europe" (170).

Like his fantasies, Boswell's role-playing represents an attempt
to relate the self to a world which exists partly in the imagination
—that is, to Corsica as it resembles Sparta or earliest Rome. When
Boswell finds himself in situations that do not demand this kind
of imaginative response, the idea of "ordinary" reality reasserts
itself; at Pino, for instance, we see him behaving at a private dinner as he would in a London tavern: "I sometimes forgot myself,
and imagining I was in a public house called for what I wanted

with the tone which one uses in calling to the waiters at a tavern. I did so at Pino ... When Signora Tomasi perceiving my mistake looked in my face and smiled, saying with much calmness and good nature, 'One thing after another, Sir' " (162). This too is a kind of involuntary fantasy, but one which recalls Boswell's usual existence in England and Scotland; this vacillation between illusion and reality, between the ordinary and imaginative levels of experience, underlies the symbolic meaning of Boswell's story.

In the same way, Boswell's attempt to understand the nature of Paoli's greatness involves a temporary participation in illusion, for seeing Paoli as a hero necessarily means entering the heroic world of his private imagination. There is in *Corsica*, as in the *Tour to the Hebrides* and the *Life of Johnson*, a strong notion of spiritual kinship between narrator and hero. The same impulse that causes Paoli to venerate the heroes of antiquity causes Boswell to venerate Paoli, and once again invites an imaginative response that is close to fantasy: "one day when I rode out, I was mounted on Paoli's own horse with rich furniture of crimson velvet, with broad gold lace, and had my guards marching along with me. ... When I returned to the Continent after all this greatness, I used to joke with my acquaintance and tell them that I could not bear to live with them, for they did not treat me with proper respect" (173). As it concerns Paoli, Boswell's role-playing is in one aspect a naive response, but in another a process of symbolic identification which momentarily collapses the distance between the ordinary man and the hero.

Eventually, though, Boswell must get down off the horse and be Boswell again. When the fantasy disintegrates we are left with the contrast between narrator and hero, between the naive enthusiasm of Boswell and the stoic greatness of Paoli. Inevitably the return to ordinary reality is accompanied by a conviction of personal inadequacy: "never was I so sensible of my own defects as while I was in Corsica. I felt how small were my abilities and how little I knew. Ambitious to be the companion of Paoli and to understand a country and a people which roused me so much, I wished to be a Sir James Macdonald" (200). There is a touch of pathos in this, for Boswell's response to the dissolution of one fantasy of personal greatness is only to indulge in another; nothing, perhaps, better illuminates the character of a narrator whose instinctive rebellion against "ordinary" reality shapes his perception of figures like Paoli and Samuel Johnson.

In the *Tour to Corsica* we see Boswell as a narrator whose own search for identity involves an unconscious wavering between the spheres of the actual and the imaginary—that is, between an idea of Corsica as a backward agrarian community governed by an obscure visionary and an alternative vision of the heroic world associated with a remote and mythic past. As a consequence the story runs a middle course between the two and portrays a reality that is neither wholly literal nor wholly imaginary. Boswell's attempt to "understand" Paoli and Corsica is finally an attempt to recover a sense of the spiritual coherence he associates with ancient myth and history. Boswell in *Corsica* is a Raphael Hythloday of the sceptical eighteenth century, whose travels take him not to a rational utopia but to a half-mythic commonwealth that recalls a simpler age of faith and order.

THREE

In the *Tour to the Hebrides,* where Samuel Johnson appears as a philosopher-hero traveling through a primitive landscape of ruined cathedrals and decaying castles, Boswell's role is in one sense purely normative—that is, he represents the ordinary traveler whose response to Highland scenes becomes the measure of Johnson's deeper and more contemplative response. Yet we have seen that the *Tour* is in a larger sense about Johnson's discovery, as a traveler, of the heroic past. Once again the major theme of the narrative derives partly from Boswell's naiveté, which here takes the form of a romantic enthusiasm for the landscape and history of the Highlands; "the very Highland names," we recall him saying of the '45, "or the sound of a bagpipe, will stir my blood, and fill me with a mixture of melancholy and respect for courage . . . in short, with a crowd of sensations with which sober rationality has nothing to do."

This is similar to the romantic impulse that shapes what we have earlier called the public perspective on Johnson as hero, for throughout the *Tour* Boswell's naive and emotional response runs as a counterpoint to Johnson's more sober rationality, supplying the imaginative context we need to understand Johnson's discovery of the heroic past. Both the normative and naïf aspects of Boswell's role are suggested in the sketch of his own character that he places close to the beginning of the *Tour:* "he was then in his thirty-third year. . . . He had thought more than any body supposed, and had a pretty good stock of general learning and knowledge. He had all Dr. Johnson's principles, with some degree of relaxation. He had rather too little, than too much prudence; and, his imagination being lively, he often said things of which the effect was very different from the intention" (V.52). In short, a Boswell similar to the Boswell who speaks in the *Tour to Corsica:* an eager and ingenuous young man whose main claim on us is his acquaintance with the hero.

In the *Tour to the Hebrides,* however, Boswell's more intimate relationship with Johnson underlies a more complex development of narrative perspective, for intimacy is a dramatic as well as a psychological principle, complicating any simple contrast between narrator and hero. We see the principle at work in the emphasis placed on Boswell's role as journalist, which is his role as creator of the story we are reading. "He presents each day's events and impressions in a totally unselfconscious way," writes Frank Brady, "a record of the normal flow of experience. At the same time, the journal is highly selfconscious, an account intended for Johnson, who read and occasionally corrected it":[8] "he asked me today how it happened that we were so little together. I told him, my Journal took up much time. Yet, on reflection, it appeared strange to me, that although I will run from one end of London to another, to pass an hour with him, I should omit to seize any spare time to be in his company, when I am settled in the same house with him. But my Journal is really a task of much time and labour, and he forbids me to contract it" (V.227).

Boswell's journal-writing involves, in the technical sense of the term, an irony, for the journal is among other things a story that is being read by its hero: "he came to my room this morning before breakfast, to read my Journal, which he has done all along. He often before said, 'I take great delight in reading it.' To-day he said, 'You improve: it grows better and better'" (V.226). This gives us the kind of internal adjustment of perspective we associate with certain types of fiction, the readiest example, perhaps, being the point in *Pamela*, close to the dénouement, where Squire B——— discovers Pamela's letters and has her continue them as a journal. The complications are obvious: we have not a story in its normal form but a story that is read by characters inside the story, whose recorded reactions then become part of the story, which is then read by those characters in the latest installment, and so on. This is precisely the problem posed by Johnson's reading of the journal that became the *Tour to the Hebrides*.

In the process, the nature of Boswell's relationship to Johnson is continuously redefined: "he read to-night, to himself, as he sat in company, a great deal of my Journal, and said to me, 'The more I read of this, I think the more highly of you'" (V.262). For in the journal Johnson is not only coming in contact with an unfamiliar version of himself—"he read this day a good deal of my Journal. . . . 'They call me a scholar, (said he,) and yet how very little literature is there in my conversation'" (V.307)— but with an unfamiliar Boswell, someone who observes and comments on his actions, who occasionally sits in partial judgment on him, and who is intrepid enough to describe even his peculiarities. Our response to every scene in which Johnson figures is complicated by the knowledge that Johnson is reading it too, even if we are left to wonder what passes through his mind: "it is remarkable," says Boswell in a footnote to his famous description of Johnson's eccentricities, "that Dr. Johnson should have read this account of some of his own peculiar habits, without saying any thing on the subject, which I hoped he would have done" (V.307*n2*).

At the same time, Johnson's reading of the journal defines the nature of his intimacy with Boswell. Johnson's comments are restricted to general praise—" 'I wish thy books were twice as big' "—and he maintains either silence or a wise neutrality toward scenes that describe his own actions. Boswell's reliance on this compound of sympathy and reserve is what allows him to use the journal as an oblique medium of communication with his hero. Devastated in an argument, for instance, he takes the day's entry as an occasion to animadvert, secure in the knowledge that Johnson will eventually read the passage. Or, when Johnson is angry with him, Boswell uses the journal as a vehicle for self-justification. Invariably Johnson reads and is silent, and in his silence we discover his sympathetic recognition of the Boswell who has "thought more than any body supposed," and who is able to view his own relationship to Johnson in a spirit of confident detachment.

Throughout the *Tour* we sense not only that Johnson recognizes Boswell's capacity for self-detachment but that he has something of an emotional dependence on it. When Johnson becomes bored or impatient and is unwilling to distress his hosts, it is Boswell who bears the brunt, uncomplainingly: "there was something not quite serene in his humour tonight . . . for he spoke of hastening away to London. . . . *Johnson.* 'Nay, I shall neither go in jest, nor stay in jest. I shall do what is fit.'—*Boswell.* 'Ay, sir, but all I desire is, that you will let me tell you when it is fit.'—*Johnson.* 'Sir, I shall not consult you' " (V.272). If Boswell passed them off less lightly, Johnson's outbursts of ill-humor might appear selfish to the point of cruelty: a man who values friendship we expect to be careful of the feelings of his friends. But Boswell does pass them off lightly, as the vagaries of a personality larger than his own, and in his easy tolerance we see the mixture of involvement and detachment that shapes his perception of Johnson as hero.

The special nature of Boswell's intimacy with Johnson, which always allows for this same mixture of involvement and detachment, also determines his mode of narration. Throughout the *Tour* the focus is on Johnson as a traveler, and the subject is in a sense the unfolding of the hero's impressions. Yet the Highland journey is a shared experience, and an account of Johnson's response must begin in Boswell's own field of perception. This double necessity becomes the basis of a distinctive descriptive rhythm: we view events first as Boswell views them, moving outward from a complex subjectivity of personal response to the more stable and "objective" context of impersonal description. At which point, usually, we discover Johnson's posture and attitude toward the same experience, which finally refers us back to the established contrast between narrator and hero. Though this rhythm controls our perspective through the *Tour* as a whole, it can often be traced in the development of a single dramatic sequence. Toward the end of the story, for instance, the travelers board a boat for Mull: Johnson is seasick and goes below; Boswell stays on deck, rejoicing in his brave role as a "stout seaman."

When a storm comes up suddenly, we view it through Boswell's eyes, in a description of men caught out at sea moving steadily toward the subjective. The sequence begins as a tiny drama of men and boats exposed suddenly to the danger of the storm: "at last it becomes so rough, and threatened to be so much worse, that Col and his servant took more courage, and said they would undertake to hit one of the harbours in Col.—'Then let us run for it in GOD's name,' said the skipper.' " But then description of the storm begins to give way to Boswell's own impressions: "but my relief was but of short duration; for I soon heard that our sails were very bad, and were in danger of being torn in pieces, in which case we should be driven upon the rocky shore of Col. . . . The perpetual talking, or rather shouting, which was carried on in Erse, alarmed me still more. A man is always suspicious of what is saying in an unknown tongue; and, if fear be his passion at the time, he grows more afraid."

Boswell's account of the storm is now an account of his own mind, running the course from simple fear to irrational suspicion to a final moment of mixed awe: "I now saw what I never saw before, a prodigious sea, with immense billows coming upon a vessel. . . . There was something grandly horrible in the sight. . . . When I thought of those who were dearest to me, and would suffer severely, should I be lost, I upbraided myself, as not having a sufficient cause for putting myself in such a danger." But as danger passes and it becomes more apparent that the boat is going to reach safety, the subjective or psychological focus is gradually replaced by an external description of events; and once the boat has reached harbor Boswell's account enlarges to include concerns driven from his mind by the danger of the storm. Only now does Johnson reappear, discovered in a posture of repose that effectively contrasts the frenzied activity of the preceding scenes: "Dr. Johnson had all this time been quiet and unconcerned. He had lain down on one of the beds, and having got free from sickness, was satisfied. . . . I now went down, with Col and Mr. Simpson, to visit him. He was lying in philosophick tranquility with a greyhound of Col's at his back, keeping him warm" (V.283).

The meaning of Johnson's repose emerges from Boswell's vivid psychological description of the effects of a storm at sea on an ordinary mind. At such moments we perceive the sense in which Boswell's mode of narration derives from his role as a normative figure, for the description of Johnson's philosophic tranquility becomes a revelation of character only because we can take Boswell's account of his own terror as a measure of normal response. This, whether the subject is a storm in the Hebrides or some scene recalling the Highland past, is the essential perspective that controls the narrative movement of the *Tour to the Hebrides:* in his role as Johnson's fellow traveler, Boswell repeatedly moves outward from a focus of purely subjective response, of immediate impressions and private imaginings, to a context of external description that includes the hero. The descriptive rhythm of the *Tour* is the literary reflection of Boswell's consciousness progressively unfolding from a direct apprehension of experience to an imaginative apprehension of the larger setting in which experience takes place.

In scenes that concern Johnson's behavior in society, Boswell's mixture of detachment and reserve also reflects his own double role as narrator and character. When Boswell is least involved psychologically—that is, when he appears simply as an onlooker— we have the perspective we associate with so many minor scenes in the *Life of Johnson,* one that shows Johnson dominating the social situation by sheer force of wit and intellect and Boswell as the spectator who adds the minimum of stage direction and external description we need to follow the action. When Boswell's psychological involvement increases, we move toward a more fully developed dramatic scene in which our implicit awareness of his reactions controls our own response. Here again the *Tour* anticipates the *Life;* in the sequence describing Johnson's meeting with Lord Monboddo, we have the same dramatic elements out of which Boswell will create the famous Johnson–Wilkes scene—a character whose views Johnson finds obnoxious and whose personality he dislikes but who finally overcomes him with politeness and friendly respect. In both scenes the suspense comes entirely from Boswell's anxiety as a character, which, recreated in retrospect, becomes the organizing principle of his account.

In Johnson's meeting with Monboddo the danger of conflict arises from his lordship's well-known opinions about man's happiness in the original state of nature. The travelers find him waiting courteously at his gate, and it is only a matter of seconds before Johnson has managed "an assault upon one of Lord Monboddo's capital dogmas"; "I was afraid," says Boswell, "there would have been a violent altercation in the very close, before we got into the house" (V.77). But over the next few pages Monboddo's unfailing politeness wins Johnson over. After a conscious effort by both men to discover a common ground of agreement, they strike upon Homer, and an extended discussion of the *Iliad* follows. By the time the dispute arises, the atmosphere is so friendly that Johnson and Monboddo can put their larger differences into the relatively harmless form of a theoretical argument about the relative happiness of a savage and a shopkeeper. Johnson emerges completely satisfied: "he was much pleased with Lord Monboddo. . . . He observed that his lordship had talked no paradoxes to-day. 'And as to the savage and the London shopkeeper, (said he,) I don't know but I might have taken the side of the savage equally, had anybody else taken the side of the shopkeeper'" (V.83).

Throughout the sequence Boswell, who has brought the meeting about, hovers on the edge of the action, fearing an outbreak of hostilities at every turn. Yet the encounter is finally a drama taking place in Boswell's mind—we perceive the imminent danger of "violent altercation" only through him—and the movement of the sequence is ultimately psychological, from anxiety to relief to satisfaction. In Boswell's description of Johnson's encounter with his father, perhaps the greatest comic sequence of the *Tour*, we have an opposite movement, but one which again places Boswell at the psychological center of the action even as he retains the literal distance of a spectator. Lord Auchinleck, like Monboddo, is a character whose beliefs run directly contrary to Johnson's own: "he was as sanguine a Whig and Presbyterian, as Dr.

Johnson was a Tory and church of England man" (V.376).
This time Boswell's anxiety as a character is absolutely central:
"I . . . begged of my friend to avoid three topicks, as to which
they differed very widely; Whiggism, Presbyterianism, and—Sir
John Pringle" (V.376). Johnson graciously agrees.

On the first day of the visit, with Johnson on his best behavior
and Lord Auchinleck doing his best to treat Johnson with respect and courtesy, things go smoothly: "it rained, and we could
not get out; but my father shewed Dr. Johnson his library. . . .
He was a sound scholar, and, in particular, had collated manu-
scripts and different editions of Anacreon . . . so that my friend
and he had much matter for conversation, without touching on
the fatal topicks of difference" (V.376). Simply by mentioning
the fatal topics Boswell heightens our sense of impending conflict, and we recognize the conversation as, at best, an uneasy
truce. Several days later, with Johnson confined to the house by
bad weather, the available list of neutral subjects is exhausted,
and behind every innocent topic lurks the danger of confrontation. It happens: "the contest began while my father was shew-
ing him his collection of medals; and Oliver Cromwell's coin
unfortunately introduced Charles the First, and Toryism. They
became exceedingly warm, and violent, and I was very much
distressed by being present at such an altercation between two
men, both of whom I reverenced; yet I durst not interfere"
(V.382).

Taken as a whole the Auchinleck sequence perfectly exemplifies the dramatic principles inherent in Boswell's double role as
narrator and character. We perceive the suspense, and the inevitable movement toward conflict, through the eyes of an emo-
tionally involved but outwardly detached spectator, much as if
we, out of sight of the stage, were listening to a running account
of a play by someone caught up in the action. But by this time
the outward course of action has become so completely identified
with the movement of Boswell's anxiety that the subject of the

sequence has become his own psychological response. Johnson, in his excitement, has forgotten about the list of "fatal topicks," and Lord Auchinleck never knew about them, so the humor of the comic denouement resides entirely in Boswell's report from the fringes of the action: "in the course of their altercation, Whiggism and Presbyterianism, Toryism and Episcopacy, were terribly buffeted. My worthy hereditary friend, Sir John Pringle, never having been mentioned, happily escaped without a bruise" (V.384).

In Johnson's encounters with Monboddo and Lord Auchinleck we are close to the perspective which, in the *Life*, allows us to see the hero both as a great man and a great eccentric, someone who at once dominates his society and yet in a sense remains outside it. Yet in the *Tour* such moments are merely comic interludes in the larger story of Johnson's discovery of a forgotten world of faith and heroes. This is the story we view through the medium of Boswell's own romantic enthusiasm for Highland scenes and which returns us to the essential contrast between narrator and hero. In the Hebrides, as in Corsica or London, Boswell represents the ordinary man in relation to the hero, and the naïf whose preoccupation with great men is part of his own search for coherence. But in the Hebrides, where both narrator and hero discover in the primitive landscape an idea of the past that exists as an alternative to the unheroic modern age, Boswell is also a storyteller who supplies the larger perspective we need to understand Johnson's Highland journey as an escape from self.

FOUR

In the *Life of Johnson*, where Johnson appears as a hero isolated from his society and age, Boswell's role as a normative figure is more complicated. In one aspect the *Life* contains a *Citizen of the World* motif, for Boswell tells his biographical story as a

Scotsman viewing English society from the outside and discovering a disturbing configuration of events and impulses that confirms his idea of Johnson as a moral hero. In the same way, Boswell coming down from Edinburgh on his annual excursion to London resembles a provincial visitor to ancient Rome; that is, England represents for him not a country merely but a cultural and imaginative ideal, and it is with this—the England of Shakespeare and Milton and Magna Carta—that he identifies Samuel Johnson. This is the symbolic perspective that allows us to see Johnson as a hero whose orthodoxy and Toryism belong to a private realm of embattled faith and whose periods of melancholy and despair represent the spiritual paralysis of a mind for which the illusion of coherence has temporarily failed.

Our idea of Johnson as hero of the *Life* depends once again on an impression of Boswell's naiveté, which in this case is an impulse toward veneration and which has the effect of transforming even ordinary scenes into symbolic episodes: "the orthodox high-church sound of the MITRE,—the figure and manner of the celebrated SAMUEL JOHNSON,—the extraordinary power and precision of his conversation, and the pride arising from finding myself admitted as his companion, produced . . . a pleasing elevation of mind beyond what I had ever before experienced" (I.401). At such moments ordinary reality is replaced by something more mysterious, for Boswell speaks as a narrator who has found an actual great man existing within the improbable confines of eighteenth-century London, and who discovers within the magic circle of his presence a moral certainty belonging to an earlier age.

As in *Corsica* and the *Tour to the Hebrides*, Boswell appears in the *Life* as a narrator whose claim on his audience derives from his personal acquaintance with the hero. But in the *Life*, a discontinuous narrative covering a great many years, personal acquaintance is no longer a simple dramatic principle that allows an unextraordinary narrator to speak with special authority about a great man. The *Life* is in one aspect the story of Boswell's friendship with Johnson—not merely of an intimate relationship but of a relationship which develops through time, which reflects changes in both narrator and hero, and which ultimately underlies the narrative movement leading to our final perception of Johnson as a figure superior to his age. Boswell's friendship with his hero is among other things a symbolic motif that allows for a changing perspective within a continuous context. This is why, when each stage of their relationship in one sense gives us a different version of Johnson as hero, we are simultaneously aware of a Johnson who is still the same.

At the same time, the *Life* is a story told retrospectively, and we are aware throughout of a Boswell who gazes back on earlier events from a fixed perspective. While Boswell portrays Johnson's early career from the viewpoint of the conventional chronicler—the invisible recorder of anecdotes, actions, and preferments —there are foreshadowings of their future intimacy: "his only amusement was in winter, when he took a pleasure in being drawn upon the ice by a boy barefooted, who pulled him along by a garter fixed around him. . . . His defective sight, indeed, prevented him from enjoying the common sports; and he once pleasantly remarked to me, 'how wonderfully well he had contrived to be idle without them' " (I.48). At such moments we hear the voice of the Boswell who will later enter Johnson's life, the sympathetic listener to whom Johnson will speak unreservedly even about the details of his painful youth. Throughout this early part of the *Life*, covering a period of fifty-four years and filled with people Boswell never knew and events he never witnessed, the story moves inevitably toward the eventual meeting of narrator and hero.

As the meeting draws nearer, Boswell by degrees abandons the viewpoint of the detached chronicler and emerges more clearly as the young Scotsman whose first impression of Johnson's greatness has come from reading his works; "at every perusal," says Boswell in his discussion of *Rasselas*, "my admiration of the mind which produced it is so highly raised, that I can scarcely believe that I had the honour of enjoying the intimacy of such a man" (I.342). This is of course a retrospective utterance, but it describes an impression of Johnson that remains a controlling idea throughout the *Life*. The Johnson who exists in the mind of the twenty-two-year-old Boswell is the idealized and almost disembodied figure who speaks with magisterial certainty about the profoundest impulses of the human heart: "I had for several years read his works . . . and had the highest reverence for their author, which had grown up in my fancy into a kind of mysterious veneration, by figuring to myself a state of solemn elevated abstraction, in which I supposed him to live in the immense metropolis of London" (V.384).

As it appeals to our normal tendency to identify an author with his works, Boswell's imaginary notion of Johnson represents a universal image, one that might be corroborated by any reader of the *Rambler* or *Rasselas*. Yet in these circumstances we also see the Boswell whose need for mystery, like his preoccupation with great men, is part of his own search for certainty. Boswell's early acquaintance with Johnson thus symbolically involves a confrontation of the real and the ideal: "it must be confessed, that his apartment, and furniture, and morning dress, were sufficiently uncouth. His brown suit of cloaths looked very rusty; he had on a little old shrivelled unpowdered wig, which was too small for his head" (V.396). The story of these first few weeks concerns Boswell's exploration of the world of actuality that surrounds Johnson, which is his attempt to accommodate the idealized to the actual: "Mr. Levet this day shewed me Dr. Johnson's library. . . . I found a number of good books, but very dusty and in great confusion. The floor was strewed with manuscript leaves, in Johnson's own hand-writing, which I beheld with a degree of veneration, supposing they perhaps might contain portions of the Rambler, or of Rasselas. . . . The place seemed to be very favourable for retirement and meditation" (I.436).

Any immediate confrontation of the idealized and the actual involves the danger of a collapse into ordinariness, if not disillusion. In the *Life* this danger passes only when Boswell's mysterious veneration of an idealized Johnson emerges as the first basis of his intimacy with the real man. For during this first period of their acquaintance, Johnson's relationship to Boswell duplicates, on the personal level, the relationship of the moralist to ordinary mankind; this is the meaning of the late-night conversations where Boswell confides his doubts about everything from theological questions to choice of career, of the great sequence that takes narrator and hero on an excursion to Greenwich to discuss Boswell's plan of study at Utrecht, and at last of the affectionate impulse that leads Johnson to oversee his young friend's departure from England: "my revered friend walked down with me to the beach, where we embraced and parted with tenderness. . . . I said, 'I hope, Sir, you will not forget me in my absence.' JOHNSON. 'Nay, Sir, it is more likely you should forget me, than that I should forget you.' As the vessel put out to sea, I kept my eyes upon him for a considerable time, while he remained rolling his majestick frame in his usual manner; and at last I perceived him walk back into the town, and he disappeared" (I.472).

Boswell's departure from England marks the end of the stage of consciousness in which real and ideal notions of Johnson combine to show forth a figure who is half a hero, half a man. When Boswell reappears in the *Life* several years later, having completed a tour of Europe that has brought him into contact with Voltaire, Rousseau, and a hundred lesser luminaries, it is with a broader and more cosmopolitan perspective; "I felt my veneration for him in no degree lessened," says Boswell, "by my having seen *multorum hominum mores et urbes.*" But there is, nonetheless, an inevitable adjustment of attitude, a movement in the direction of tentativeness and reserve: "the roughness, indeed, which sometimes appeared in his manners, was more striking to me now, from my having been accustomed to the studied smooth complying habits of the Continent; and I clearly recognized in him, not without respect for his honest conscientious zeal, the same indignant and sarcastical mode of treating every attempt to unhinge or weaken good principles" (II.13–14).

This represents a second period of danger in their relationship, for Boswell's new cosmopolitanism involves not simply a changed perception of Johnson's character but an easy tolerance of attitudes that Johnson regards as intolerable. And of the people associated with them: " 'it seems, Sir, you have kept very good company abroad, Rousseau and Wilkes!' . . . "My dear Sir, you don't call Rousseau bad company. Do you really think *him* a bad man?' JOHNSON. 'Sir, if you are talking jestingly of this, I don't talk with you. If you mean to be serious, I think him one of the worst of men, a rascal, who ought to be hunted out of society, as he has been' " (II.11). Boswell's cosmopolitanism is at this point a kind of innocence, for he fails to discern in such outbursts the larger meaning of Johnson's conflict with the Enlightenment and his growing isolation from his age. The Boswell who left England a pupil and disciple has returned in some partial sense an adversary.

Yet Boswell's exposure to the European philosophes has in fact laid the groundwork for the middle period of his relationship with Johnson. In the years that follow his return, Boswell comes to recognize the social and political doctrines of the philosophes as threats to his own deep need for moral certainty. As it becomes clear that his cultivation of great men has been indiscriminate, that figures like Voltaire and Rousseau do belong to a party which has mounted a powerful attack on the foundations of traditional belief, Boswell begins to view Johnson in a new way. Earlier, it might be said, the conflict between the actual and the idealized existed largely in Boswell's mind, as a conflict among his own varying impressions of Johnson. In the middle period this gives way to Boswell's more mature and stable perception of Johnson as a man who is himself caught between the real and

the ideal levels of human existence—that is, as a hero in an unheroic world. It is during this middle period, which occupies by
far the greater part of the *Life,* that Johnson's character as hero
is defined.

Boswell's changed perception of Johnson reflects a change in
his own consciousness and involves a certain sacrifice: "I missed
that aweful reverence," says Boswell at one point, "with which
I used to contemplate MR. SAMUEL JOHNSON, in the complex
magnitude of his literary, moral, and religious character. I have
a wonderful superstitious love of *mystery;* when, perhaps, the
truth is, that it is owing to the cloudy darkness of my own mind"
(III.225). But the loss of the idealized Johnson who lived in
Boswell's imagination when he came to London as a young man
is compensated by his more mature conception of Johnson as a
hero whose authority derives from the process of spiritual struggle and whose painfully earned allegiance to traditional belief
offers comfort to lesser men. This is a deeper mystery, and one
which makes Johnson the central figure in Boswell's own search
for certainty; it is in this sense that the *Life* is, as Bertrand Bronson has written, "the almost involuntary tribute of a great human
weakness to a great human strength."[9] Thus through the greater
part of the *Life* we see Boswell as a narrator whose anxieties
(melancholy, religious doubts) run parallel to Johnson's on the
ordinary level and whose refuge in traditional values (Toryism,
orthodoxy) is the same.

Here once again we are dealing with that notion of spiritual
kinship between narrator and hero which is a normal feature of
Boswellian narrative: in the *Life* Boswell appears as an ordinary
man sustained not by Johnson's solutions to moral anxiety but
by Johnson's struggle, on the heroic level, with similar anxieties.
This gives us the Boswell who, throughout the long middle period of his acquaintance with Johnson, turns to his friend again
and again for a special kind of reassurance: "it was most comfortable to me to experience, in Dr. Johnson's company, a relief

from this uneasiness. His steady vigorous mind held firm before me those objects which my own feeble and tremulous imagination frequently presented, in such a wavering state, that my reason could not judge well of them" (III.193). This is reassurance by heroic example, and at such moments Johnson's own tendency to melancholy and despair becomes in one sense immaterial, in another the source of his power to dissipate, by his very presence, the anxieties of ordinary men.

Beneath the crowded social drama of the middle years—the dinners at Streatham, the journeys to Oxford and Lichfield, the meetings of the Club—lie the simpler outlines of a symbolic situation described earlier. Johnson appears as the genuine moral hero of whom the idealized philosopher-moralist is only a public counterpart, Boswell as the narrator who discovers in his hero's affirmation of traditional values a possibility of coherence unperceived by lesser men. We see this most typically when narrator and hero are alone: "he asked me to go up to his study with him, where we sat a long while together, sometimes in silence, and sometimes conversing . . . my respectful attention never abated, and my wish to hear him was such, that I constantly watched every dawning of communications from that great and illuminated mind" (II.357). Boswell's reverential tone directs us, here as elsewhere, to the guiding principle of his mature relationship with Johnson: if, beyond the troubled reality of an unspiritual age, an invisible and timeless order of coherence does exist, it can only be known through someone like Johnson.

At the same time, this perception of Johnson as hero inevitably involves a sense of his isolation from his age, an awareness that his reassuring orthodoxy represents a merely personal system of beliefs which were at one time universal. This is why, when we think of the world of the *Life of Johnson*, we are really contemplating a world within a world, one transformed by Johnson's presence and symbolically associated with his values; thus we have, for instance, the context in which Boswell sees a simple jaunt to Lichfield as a pilgrimage: "we put up at the Three Crowns . . . the very next house to that in which Johnson was born and brought up. . . . We had a comfortable supper, and got into high spirits. I felt all my Toryism glow in this old capital of Staffordshire. I could have offered incense *genio loci*" (II.461). The same principle applies to people: as London is the center of a Johnsonian world that radiates outward toward Oxford and Lichfield, Burke, Goldsmith, Reynolds, and others are near the center of a "Johnson circle" that, having a personal and moral periphery, exists apart from society as a whole.

The nature of Boswell's intimacy with Johnson, the intimacy of the ordinary man with the hero, places him at the very center of this circle, and in the position from which he describes Johnson during the middle period of the *Life*. Here once again the idea of veneration reflects both the normative and the naïf aspects of Boswell's role as narrator and represents a claim to a special kind of knowledge; after giving an account of his stay with Johnson at Ashbourne in 1777, Boswell inserts into the *Life* Sir William Forbes's reaction to his original journal: " 'I derive more benefit from Dr. Johnson's admirable discussions than I should be able to draw from his personal conversation; for I suppose there is not a man in the world to whom he discloses his sentiments so freely as to yourself' " (III.208). It is finally because Johnson recognizes Boswell's veneration as a genuine need for moral reassurance, and unhesitatingly accepts it as such, that Boswell is able to penetrate to the last region of intimacy, one inaccessible to men who, like Burke or Reynolds or Goldsmith, see Johnson in a different light.

It is during the middle period of Boswell's friendship with Johnson, during the years when narrator and hero sustain this special relationship, that the nature of Johnson's heroism is defined. This is why, within the framework of the narrative as a whole, we notice a certain symmetry of parts: the early period of the *Life*, beginning with Boswell's detached account of Johnson's youth and ending with his own departure from England, and the final period, beginning with Johnson's decline and ending with his death, stand in relation to the middle period as prologue and epilogue do to the main action of a play. The story of the *Life*, properly speaking, is the story of those years when Boswell, on his journeys down to London from Edinburgh, is conscious of arriving in a world from which, as long as it contains Johnson, the possibility of moral certainty and spiritual coherence has not yet disappeared.

The final period begins in a gradual reassertion of distance, as Boswell becomes aware that this self-contained world, so long sustained by Johnson's commanding presence, has begun to pass away. Now Johnson appears almost as a survivor of an earlier age, and Boswell as the sharer of his memories: "we stopped a little while by the rails of the Adelphi, looking on the Thames, and I said to him with some emotion that I was now thinking of two friends we had lost, who once lived in the buildings behind us, Beauclerk and Garrick. 'Ay, Sir (said he, tenderly) and two such friends as cannot be supplied' " (IV.99). It is during the final period that Johnson's isolation, which has earlier been moral and symbolic, becomes actual and that Boswell begins to describe his hero as posterity might see him. Here again we have a strong sense of underlying symmetry, for Boswell's detachment now is personal and almost elegiac, the corollary and complement of the formal, self-imposed detachment with which his narrative began.

As Johnson appears more and more as someone half belonging to another world, and as the intimate perspective of the middle period gives way to the public or elegiac perspective of the last years, Boswell himself appears in a different light, as a narrator whose relationship with his hero is colored by a sense of impending loss; as when he calls on Johnson before going back to Edinburgh in 1783: "he embraced me, and gave me his blessing, as usual when I was leaving him for any length of time. I walked from his door to-day, with a fearful apprehension of what might

happen before I returned" (IV.226). Such moments foreshadow
not merely Johnson's death but the final lonely position from
which Boswell will tell his story. For the retrospective dimension
of Boswell's narrative, which shapes his story from the opening
pages to the end, derives from his own role as ultimate survivor,
someone who has lived to see the passing of a hero who survived,
by some few years, the passing of his own world.

Boswell's sense of himself as a survivor controls the scene that
so movingly describes his final parting from Johnson in 1784.
The scene is a triumph of emotional understatement, one which
hides its ultimate sadness beneath a routine attendance to concrete details of time and place—"I accompanied him to Sir Joshua
Reynolds' coach, to the entry of Bolt-court. He asked me whether I would not go with him to his house; I declined it, from an
apprehension that my spirits would sink" (IV.338–39)—but
which already shows Boswell moving into the area of retrospective reverence from which he will portray Johnson as a universal
figure. In this moment of leave-taking we see Johnson as someone who is shrunken as a man, already growing as a memory:
"when he had got down upon the foot-pavement, he called out,
'Fare you well;' and without looking back, sprang away with a
kind of pathetick briskness, if I may use that expression, which
seemed to indicate a struggle to conceal uneasiness, and impressed
me with a foreboding of our long, long, separation."

Toward the end of the *Life* Boswell, as he entered the story
late, takes his leave early: "I now relieve the readers of this
Work from any further personal knowledge of its authour; who,
if he should be thought to have obtruded himself too much upon
their attention, requests them to consider the peculiar plan of
biographical undertaking" (IV.380). The rest of the *Life*, including the description of Johnson's last days and of his death,
is drawn from the accounts of witnesses, and Boswell's is again,
as it was at the very beginning of the narrative, the voice of the
detached chronicler. Yet the formality of Boswell's tone as he

withdraws himself from the story, and the sense of completed symmetry we have when we watch him resume the role in which he began, disguise the deeper and more personal meaning of the ceremony. Boswell's early leave-taking is the assertion of a final distance, one that aligns him with us in his separation from Johnson and that unites him with us in a shared vision of Johnson as hero.

When Boswell takes his leave of us we are once again reminded, perhaps more strongly than at any earlier point, that the *Life of Johnson* has been in large part a drama taking place in the mind of its creator, and that Johnson emerges from it a hero because he exists in the perception of a storyteller whose doubts and fears and moral anxieties so closely resemble those that have come to dominate the age we have agreed to call modern. If the story of Boswell's long and intimate acquaintance with Johnson symbolically recalls the older and simpler relationship of the ordinary man to the hero of quest or struggle, it nonetheless revolves around an inward principle of heroic indomitability that belongs distinctively to a time in which all things are in doubt. The Johnson we meet in the pages of the *Life* is a universal figure because Boswell's own search for spiritual certainty, the search which in his story so inevitably leads him to acquaintance and then to friendship with Johnson, is itself a universal one.

4

PHILOSOPHICK HEROISM
THE *LIFE OF JOHNSON*

THE *Life of Johnson*, viewed in the light of a larger concern with Boswell's conception of the hero, might be described as a tragedy taking place inside a comedy. The description of course applies to what we have been calling the principle of generic tension in Boswellian narrative, for as the tragedy is the story of Johnson's spiritual struggle, its scene is an inner world of doubt and suffering and embattled resolve. This is the world we glimpse in the *Prayers and Meditations* and in certain of Johnson's private conversations and is properly the world in which he appears as a heroic figure. Then, beyond the immediate perimeter of Johnson's inward conflict, there exists a sharply contrasting scene— the bustling and seemingly complacent world of late eighteenth-century England, the world we encounter in the novels of Fielding and Smollett or the comedies of Sheridan and Goldsmith. If Johnson in one sense seems at home in this sphere of teeming actuality, he in another sense moves in it as an alien, a figure from Sophoclean or Shakespearean tragedy who has strayed into the pages of *Tom Jones*.

The sense in which the characters and dramatic episodes of the *Life* belong mostly to the comic world is evident even in its topography. The central locale of the story is London, which has in Boswell's writing the same significance it has in Ben Jonson's comedies or Dickens's novels, as a microcosm of English society comprehending (as Boswell once says) "the whole of human life in all its variety, the contemplation of which is inexhaustible."

This is the London of eighteenth-century satire and comic fiction, a milieu of shops and coffeehouses and crowded streets, and an endless spectacle of the diversity produced by a commercial age: "JOHNSON. 'Why, Sir, Fleet-street has a very animated appearance; but I think the full tide of human existence is at Charing-cross.'" And beyond London lies the peaceful landscape we glimpse on Johnson's annual jaunts into the countryside, the landscape of an older England enjoying, in Jeffrey Hart's phrase, "a long Indian summer," a leisurely age of "coaches and inns, rubicund squires with their foxes and port, trim Georgian buildings and pleasant squares."[1]

Such a world is not necessarily comic, but in some fundamental sense it encourages and sustains comedy, repudiates tragedy. This is why, in observing the similarities between the *Life* and the eighteenth-century comic novel or comedy of manners, we are really dealing with a generic convention, one which normally associates comedy with a scene resembling ordinary life and tragedy with a more abstract realm of high passion and stark inevitability. For tragedy and comedy imitate different levels of human experience, and convention is in this case another name for mimetic integrity: the tragic hero does not sit down to eat roast beef, or get involved in schemes for making money, because he inhabits a world where the tavern and the stock exchange have no real existence. And in the crowded world of comedy, where men eat and argue and read the newspapers, tragedy itself seems unreal.

The *Life of Johnson* gives us a hero who does sit down to eat roast beef, and who moreover consumes it with the gustatorial abandon of a Squire Western. This is one of the major complications of Boswell's narrative: whenever we see Johnson wholly participating in the world of actuality that surrounds him—and he has a large sense of comedy and a huge appetite for the real—he becomes something of a comic figure. Consider, for instance, Johnson's eccentricities, those curious beliefs and moments of odd behavior of which the nineteenth century made so much: these belong precisely to the area of Johnson's participation in the comic world and are recognizably the traits of the eighteenth-century humor character, of Sir Roger de Coverley or Parson Adams or Matthew Bramble. The *Life* most resembles a comedy of manners when Johnson appears in this light, having temporarily taken on the coloring of his surroundings.

When the *Life* comes to deal with the darker side of Johnson's existence, the story moves to the opposite extreme, toward a bleak and separate world of spiritual isolation. At such times the movement and bustle of the scene in the foreground seem almost to have become suspended, and we find ourselves tracing what is in effect a submerged story. This is the part of the *Life* which is about the moral struggle of a great man and which reminds us so often of Greek or Shakespearean tragedy. And by the same token, this is the part of the *Life* we normally have in mind when we speak of Johnson as a hero, for when we focus on the themes associated with Johnson's inner conflict—his melancholy, his fear of death, his deep religious anxiety—we temporarily leave behind the comic and anecdotal side of Boswell's narrative, the drawing room scenes and teatime conversations and encounters with minor characters, and enter the lonely sphere of Johnson's private struggle.

Yet while the *Life* seems to invite us to respond separately to the comic and tragic portions of Johnson's story, it finally asks us to see the separation as an illusion and to understand the menace that actually lies behind the happily complacent eighteenth-century world it portrays. For Johnson's personal struggle is the central drama of the *Life,* and in contemplating it we begin to see this world in a kind of double focus: viewed from its own level, it seems innocent and peaceful enough, but viewed from a higher plane of spiritual coherence and heroic endeavor, it becomes a frightening place. Johnson is a tragic figure precisely because he inhabits a world where comedy, with its embrace of the external and avoidance of the inner or spiritual, is the only possibility left. In such a world the man of heroic temperament exists apart.

The tragedy of Johnson's existence begins in his isolation, for his is an age which, as Carlyle put it, denies the desirableness of great men, and which does so from a fundamentally self-protective impulse. English society as it is portrayed in the *Life* represents, just beneath its surface of busy optimism, a very image of what Carlyle called "common languid Times, with their unbelief, distress, perplexity," where belief in its traditional forms is in the process of disintegration and where moral purpose and largeness of spirit are only an embarrassment to the beholder. This is why Boswell, as he seeks to make Johnson's heroism comprehensible, so often gazes backward to an ideal past in which the hero and his society existed within a common framework of shared concern and where the great man was an object not of embarrassment but of admiration.

In this aspect the drama of the *Life* is one in which the hero and his society have found radically different responses to the same terrifying possibility, for behind the spiritual disintegration of the age lies the specter of "necessity"—not the Divine necessity of the Calvinists but the necessity of science and empirical philosophy, one which threatens all creeds impartially and denies the existence of the free self. Caught in this web of circumstance, ordinary men can only give in to moral paralysis—"the advancing tide of matter," in Huxley's words, "threatens to drown their souls, the tightening grip of law impedes their freedom"—or seek refuge in the world of the actual and the comprehensible, where there is still room for optimism. But for Johnson, portrayed as a man of superior vision and heroic temperament, there is no choice but struggle.

This specter of necessity is one which Carlyle, in his essay on the *Life*, correctly identifies as a kind of spiritual death: "all this that thou hast so often heard about 'force of circumstances' . . .

wherein thou, as in a nightmare Dream, sittest paralyzed, and hast no force left,—was in very truth . . . little other than a hag-ridden vision of death-sleep." The *Life* places Johnson in a world where "the supposition of an eternal necessity without design," as Boswell calls it in the *Tour to the Hebrides,* haunts the further fringes of conventional belief, which is why we see behind Johnson's melancholy and religious anxiety not just a fear of damnation but a fear that damnation may not exist. For Hell implies the existence of Heaven, and there is an ontological comfort in doubts about salvation, at least when the alternative is the possibility that the material universe is the blind and relentless enemy of consciousness and that the immortality of the soul is an illusion born of human weakness.

Yet the *Life* also pictures a world where belief is still possible, where infidelity still goes abroad disguised as scepticism and pays formal deference to religion. This situation was to change in the next century—one thinks of Charlotte Brontë's horrified reaction to a recent book: "it is the first exposition of avowed atheism and materialism I have ever read. . . . If this be the Truth, man or woman who beholds her can but curse the day he or she was born"[2]—but the *Life* shows us an age that has just begun to recognize the subversive implications of Newton's science and Locke's empiricism, to realize that the scepticism of Hume and Voltaire is the enemy of faith as well as superstition, and to perceive that the doctrine of man's natural goodness, preached by Rousseau and a hundred minor philosophes, has fatally reversed the Christian myth of the Fall. But though the direction of the tide may be discerned, it has not yet swept away the foundations of old belief, and there is still the possibility of resistance.

Johnson's real conflict in the *Life* is not with the philosophes and freethinkers who appear in his conversation as abstract adversaries, but with the message of profound despair that is cloaked by their optimistic rationalism. Our own accommodation of Enlightenment doctrines perhaps makes it difficult to understand why Boswell saw Johnson's resistance to intellectual change as a kind of moral heroism, something concerned less with religious or political notions than with the final annihilation of the self. But it *is* heroic: "natural laws," as Pater said, "we shall never modify, embarrass us as they may; but there is still something in the nobler or less noble attitude with which we watch their fatal combinations." Again and again in the *Life* we see Boswell, full of his own deep moral anxiety, going to Johnson for comfort; and he always comes away strengthened, not by Johnson's ritual exposition of some familiar article of belief (though that usually provides the occasion) but by the spectacle of a mind that refuses utterly to give in to hopelessness. Boswell's doubts represent those of ordinary men, and Johnson's strength is the strength of the hero. One thinks, in these scenes, of Matthew Arnold's lines:

> Yet now, when boldest wills give place,
> When Fate and Circumstance are strong,
> And in their rush the human race
> Are swept, like huddling sheep, along;
>
> Those sterner spirits let me prize,
> Who, though the tendence of the whole
> They less than us might recognize,
> Kept, more than us, their strength of soul.

Though it affords comfort to weaker souls, Johnson's brave orthodoxy is always seen in the *Life* as something associated with his conscious role as spokesman for traditional belief. Behind the public certainty there is a world of private doubt, and we always sense that Johnson does see, with a kind of tragic clairvoyance, the tendence of the whole. This is why we so often find him refuting some apparently innocent doctrine: " 'in this book it is maintained that virtue is natural to man, and that if we would but consult our own hearts, we should be virtuous. Now after consulting our own hearts all we can, and with all the helps we have, we find how few of us are virtuous. This is saying a thing which all mankind know not to be true' " (III.352). For Johnson contends with such ideas on their level of final implication, and in his remarks we glimpse his allegiance to a vision of human existence for which doctrine only provides a metaphor—"the assertions of Christianity," Huxley once said, "when freed from their mythological incrustations . . . happen unfortunately to be true. Our universe is the universe of Behemoth and Leviathan, not of Helvétius and Godwin."

In the eighteenth-century world of the *Life* such a vision of the universe is already becoming anomalous, not because the new doctrines have triumphed but because men, in their confusion, have turned away from matters of ultimate belief. This is the beginning of spiritual disintegration and of Boswell's image of English society, a society where the great conflicts of principle that once led to civil war have degenerated into the venality of party politics, where class distinctions are disappearing in the flux of social mobility introduced by trade and progress, where wars are fought at a distance remote from the life of the ordinary citizen, for reasons best understood by the monopolists and the ministers who serve them. And beyond this lies the threat of actual social dissolution: there are the occasional outbursts of mob rule, an aristocracy given over to foppery, an organized movement to circumscribe further the prerogatives of the rightful monarch, and the infidel philosophy imported from France, with its English sympathizers. The world is in disarray, and the universe of Helvétius and Godwin is replacing the universe of Behemoth and Leviathan almost silently.

An age in transition is entirely comfortable with neither the new nor the old, and Johnson's relationship with his society is ambivalent. In turning away from the larger concerns of the spirit, English society has inevitably become (in Newman's phrase) the purgatory of great men, the notion of greatness being now only an embarrassing reminder of times when life encouraged high belief and noble action. Yet the superior man is also a symbol of the free and realized self, and in a time of general dismay his resistance becomes a token of hope; this is what Disraeli had in mind when, in the following century, he lamented that "individuality is dead; there is a want of inward and personal energy in man; and that is what people feel and mean when they go about complaining there is a want of faith."[3] Boswell portrays a society which is simply confused by the idea of greatness and which gazes only half comprehendingly at the moral struggle of the isolated great man.

For the hero living in an unheroic age is necessarily an isolated figure. In a time of spiritual disintegration, when lesser men have turned to lesser things, the superior man is left to evolve from his own knowledge and intuitions the structure of belief that supplies the meaning of his existence. But the effort, tragically, begins and ends in his own mind: in the *Life* Johnson defends his private system of values so often and so convincingly that we are sometimes tempted to forget this, to see him not as an isolated hero but as the spokesman for an order actually existing in society. But this is an illusion, for Johnson's principles—what Boswell calls his Toryism and his orthodoxy—belong not to the reality of eighteenth-century England but to the medium of idealized tradition through which he views the world. To mistake this point is to see Johnson merely as a defender of the ancien régime and to ignore the pathos of his personal struggle.

Johnson's great effort is to impose a comprehensible order on existence in a society where all principles of order seem to be disappearing and where the self-creating intellect is the only remaining ally in the battle for spiritual survival. This brings us to the central principle of Johnson's thought, which is projection— a movement that begins in pure self-knowledge and moves outward toward total generalization. We have seen how he argues with the theory that virtue is natural to man: "after consulting our own hearts all we can, and with all the helps we have, we find how few of us are virtuous. This is saying a thing which all mankind know not to be true." Behind nearly every sentence

Johnson utters in the *Life* is the notion that the individual stands as a microcosm of human nature and that moral knowledge begins not in abstract ethical or social theory but in close examination of the self. If the examination is honest, rigorous, and courageous, it will lead to conclusions true to the facts of all human existence.

This method of reasoning places the individual at the center of the moral and ethical universe, and it contains a large potential for error: if one is committed to generalizing what is merely personal and perhaps unique, an entire system of values will be erected on one grand fallacy. This danger is present in the *Life* and forms part of the drama of the conversational scenes; again and again we see Johnson universalizing some aspect of his own experience, and when he arrives at a conclusion that commands our assent, it is because we have recognized ourselves in what he says. Johnson's authority as a moralist rests ultimately on the courage and honesty with which he has faced himself and discovered in his own existence principles that are permanent and universal. The *Life* appeals to the judgment of its audience in much the same way as a play does, for Boswell presents Johnson's sayings not as fixed sententiae but as continuous dramatic evidence inviting us to share his perception of the hero as a superior man.

A second danger is more discomfiting: the process of universalizing one's own experience involves another kind of subjectivity, one which cannot be conquered even by perfect honesty, for it arises from the very nature of the mind as a separate entity— so many men, in other words, and so many systems of belief. This is why Johnson's view of reality appeals ultimately to the test of traditional belief, for the history of the human intellect is one in which any number of such systems have jostled and conflicted, until (in a kind of dialectical process) differences have dissolved and a correct order has been established by the collective testimony of human experience. This is also the light in which we should view Johnson's orthodoxy, which is seen in the *Life* not as restricting and conventional but as liberating and enlightening: if one reasons aright, one will after all only reach conclusions that men have reached before and that will earn the symbolic sanction of evolved wisdom.

Yet the same principles which establish Johnson's authority as a moralist, and which confirm our impression of his superiority to other men, are finally insufficient to answer his spiritual needs. For the moralist, in his role as an observer who stands apart from society and remarks its vanity and folly, is by nature an unintegrated figure, and the *Life* always maintains a sharp distinction between the magisterial certainty of Johnson's public pronouncements, which we associate with the voice that speaks to us in the *Rambler* or *Rasselas*, and the world of private doubt and anguish revealed in the *Prayers and Meditations*. Johnson's deepest concern is with the ultimate shape of things, and we always sense his need for a kind of spiritual coherence that perhaps passed away with the world of Aquinas and Augustine, a world in which belief was inseparable from thought and the finest endeavors of the human mind celebrated a reality that lay eternally beyond the self.

This interplay of public certainty and private doubt is the major theme of Johnson's personal drama and more than anything else defines his character as hero. In Johnson the defender of orthodoxy and tradition, fighting a solitary battle for coherence and belief, we have the hero as Carlyle conceived of him, one "who lives in the inward sphere of things, in the True, Divine and Eternal: his being is in that; he declares that abroad, by act or speech as it may be, in declaring himself abroad." Yet Johnson's struggle, which begins in a reasoning outward from self, ends finally in a return to self, for the principles that govern human existence do not govern the universe. Johnson's private structure of coherence represents a courageous attempt to embrace everything from English politics to revealed doctrine, but

In the *Life* this symbolic context is absent, for eighteenth-century society has lost all idea of heroic endeavor; its false worship of commercial magnates and unscrupulous politicians in fact has, as in Fielding's *Jonathan Wild* or Gay's *Beggar's Opera*, made the concept of the great man a popular joke. So Boswell's portrayal of Johnson begins in a notion of superiority that is already abstract, even disembodied. Johnson's career as a writer is a counterpart to heroic activity, but in Boswell this is of minor import: the purpose of the *Life* is not to exalt the profession of authorship but to tell the story of a moral hero who happens to be an author. In the final analysis Johnson's superiority is of the sort we first met in Boswell's portrait of Paoli—a quality that reveals itself most strongly in the actual personality of the hero. This is why the *Life* so often takes us into Johnson's presence.

Yet Boswell's concept of superiority, in all its abstraction, is specific enough, for it means intellectual superiority. The *Life* begins with the grand assumption that the life of man is the life of the mind and that men possessed of superior minds are in effect superior beings. (Here begins the notion of the "Johnson circle," where a man like Burke is acknowledged less for his talents as a statesman than for his powers as a thinker and conversationalist.) Thus we see Johnson's potentiality for greatness even in his youth: "that superiority over his fellows, which he maintained with so much dignity in his march through life, was not assumed from vanity and ostentation, but was the natural and constant effect of those extraordinary powers of mind, of which he could not but be conscious by comparison; the intellectual difference . . . being as clear in his case as the superiority of stature in some men above others" (I.47). The effect of this is to place the center of symbolic values where Boswell wants it: the question of whether being the author of the *Rambler* is really as important as being, say, a general or a prime minister is removed from the category of relevant questions one may ask about the *Life*.

Boswell's judgment is not enough, however, for the values of a biographer may be arbitrary or eccentric: the author of a *Life of Johnson* may simply be a misguided soul who happens to prefer lexicographers to warriors and kings. This is why the *Life* so often emphasizes the "submission and deference" accorded Johnson by those who know him personally; again, the theme begins in youth, as when Johnson's schoolfellows "come in the morning as his humble attendants, and carry him to school. One in the middle stooped, while he sat upon his back, and one on each side supported him; and thus he was borne triumphant. Such a proof of the early predominance of intellectual vigour is very remarkable, and does honour to human nature" (I.47–48). This is a domestic version of the triumph of the hero, born out of an instinctive reverence for the quality of greatness. Out of such scenes the *Life* creates the image of a society which, in its immediate relation to Johnson, enlarges and verifies Boswell's perception of his natural superiority to other men.

When Johnson has come to London and begun to establish his fame as an author, the theme of intellectual superiority becomes more direct and concrete. But even Boswell's portrayal of Johnson's literary career retains the emphasis on a more abstract concept of personal greatness, one that finds only partial expression in his written works. We are seldom told merely that Johnson composed such a work in such a year (except for minor works) but also that it was done in a burst of energy of which few men would be capable. As with the *Rambler:* "posterity will be astonished when they are told . . . that many of these discourses, which we should suppose had been laboured with all the slow attention of literary leisure, were written in haste as the moment pressed, without even being read over by him before they were printed" (I.203). Or "The Vanity of Human Wishes": "the fervid rapidity with which it was produced, is scarcely credible. I have heard him say, that he composed seventy lines of it in one day, without putting one of them upon paper till they were finished" (I.192).

The great example of this kind of exaltation of Johnson's powers is, of course, Boswell's reverential discussion of the *Dictionary*, which as a work of creative scholarship represents an heroic accomplishment. Among Johnson's major works the *Dictionary* has a special significance, for the *Life* as a whole posits language and its arts (including conversation) as the most important achievement of civilization, and the *Dictionary* has made Johnson monarch over these things. But Boswell always makes us aware of the spiritual struggle behind the accomplishment: the final importance of the *Dictionary* is not that it represents the work of an entire French or Italian academy but that it was carried on in time taken out from lethargy and despair. This is always the point when Boswell talks about Johnson's bursts of literary energy, for at a certain point even the most superhuman effort takes on its value because of Johnson's gigantic disinclination to exert himself at all. Johnson's greatest works are not only testimony to his superiority of mind but concrete symbols of his victory over himself.

The story of Johnson's literary career returns us therefore to the larger theme of spiritual isolation, for this is what shapes Boswell's perception of his hero as an author whose personal greatness is only partly realized in his works and whose considerable literary achievement absorbed only a fraction of his energies. A question arises about the remainder, and the *Life* gives us, in dramatic form, an answer sharply different from Johnson's own. For Johnson, in those gloomy periods when he is unable to work, accuses himself (in the special meaning he gives to the word) of dissipation, and we always reject the explanation as being too severe—if it were not, the effect would be to shrink Johnson's stature as hero: we do not give our admiration to a man who is an actual moral weakling. The other answer, one which is more positive and reassuring, and which occupies the greatest scenes of the *Life*, lies in Johnson's escape into company and conversation.

Johnson in conversation is the image of a man of superlative powers exercising them in an area just outside his proper calling, and the image is a dramatic affirmation of Boswell's concept of greatness as an abstract quality. In every magnificently rounded sentence Johnson utters in the *Life*, we hear the voice of a great man who cannot, even in so unpromising a situation as social talk, cease being great. If Johnson, with his stern sense of moral duty, sees these hours in the tavern and drawing room as a kind of dissipation, the *Life* pictures them as an alternative theater of intellectual superiority. For Boswell, appealing to the tendency of all of us to confuse the literary persona of a writer with his actual personality, represents Johnson's conversation as an extension of his literary art, and takes both as symbolic aspects of a single magnitude of personal character. After Johnson's reputation as an author is established, and his authority as a moralist embraces both his talk and his writings, the *Life* treats his fame as a conversationalist as a kind of literary fame, the deference paid to Johnson in social situations being an immediate analogue to the homage posterity pays to the great writer.

Like his writings, however, Johnson's conversation gives us only a partial idea of his actual superiority, and the *Life* reminds us again and again that Johnson's greatness is something that can be fully comprehended only by those who move in his presence. In Johnson's later life the anonymous Lichfield boys who once carried him to school are replaced by more distinguished company, but the theme of social deference is the same. Consider Langton's description of a typical scene: "among the gentlemen were Lord Althorpe . . . Lord Macartney, Sir Joshua Reynolds, Lord Lucan, Mr. Wraxal, whose book you have probably seen . . . Dr. Warren, Mr. Pepys, the Master in Chancery . . . and Dr. Bernard, the Provost of Eton. As soon as Dr. Johnson was come in and had taken a chair, the company began to collect round him, till they became not less than four, if not five, deep; those behind standing, and listening over the heads of those that were sitting near him" (III.425–26).

The company which surrounds Johnson in such scenes forms

a kind of microsociety, one which has rediscovered the principle
of personal superiority in the unlikely setting of an eighteenth-
century drawing room and which accords Johnson the deference
that men conventionally pay to a leader or chief. As the *Life*
progresses, and more and more people pass in and out of the
magic circle of Johnson's presence, this society expands to the
point that we begin to think of it as a self-enclosed world, one
composed of authors, noblemen, statesmen, tradesmen, and pros-
titutes, and held together by a common perception of Johnson
as a superior man. This is why the *Life* so often returns to a certain type of scene, showing us a situation in which social distinctions dissolve and social forms are abandoned, and Johnson alone
commands the attention of the company.

At the center of the society which acknowledges Johnson's
superiority is the circle of famous men, including such figures as
Burke, Goldsmith, Reynolds, and Gibbon, whose public deference to Johnson is the highest proof of his moral and intellectual
stature. Every reader of the *Life* will recall, for instance, the incident of Goldsmith's epitaph, where the members of this circle
agree among themselves on certain emendations to the inscrip-
tion Johnson has composed for Goldsmith's tomb: "but the question was, who should have the courage to propose them to him?
At last it was hinted, that there could be no way so good as that
of a *Round Robin*, as the sailors call it, which they make use of
when they enter into a conspiracy, so as not to let it be known
who puts his name first or last to the paper" (III.84). The episode is of course half comic, but underlying the jeu d'esprit there
is a serious deference to Johnson's authority, proving, "in the
strongest manner, the reverence and awe with which Johnson
was regarded, by some of the most eminent men of his time, in
various departments, and even by such of them as lived most
with him" (III.85).

When it is seen in the light of episodes like this one, Boswell's
own veneration of Johnson dissolves into the general atmosphere

of "reverence and awe" that surrounds his hero, and we hear him as a spokesman for the community which has taken Johnson as its center. There is more to our perception of Johnson's superiority than the scenes in the *Life* that dwell explicitly on the theme of social deference, of course, but they are the dramatic evidence which allows Boswell to move outward to more subtle affirmations of Johnson's character as a superior man, supplying an objective correlative to the metaphors, similes, and allusions that shape Boswell's description of other scenes. Consider Boswell's account of an ordinary dinner at his friend Dilly's, where Johnson sits down with a "Mr. Capel Lofft, who, though a most zealous Whig, has a mind so full of learning and knowledge . . . and withal so much liberality, that the stupendous powers of the literary Goliath, though they did not frighten this little David of popular spirit, could not but excite his admiration" (IV.278).

Boswell's allusion to the biblical fable is made half in jest, but in speaking of Johnson's "stupendous powers" he is entirely serious. One of the more reliable comic motifs of the *Life* concerns the entrance onstage of characters who assert themselves in Johnson's presence, either through zeal (as with Mr. Capel Lofft), or heedless self-pride (Goldsmith), or ignorant familiarity (Johnson's old schoolfellow Mr. Edwards), and the comedy always depends on our graver notion of Johnson's real superiority. For when Boswell speaks of the "fear" and "awe" that Johnson inspires, or the "courage" it takes to contend with him in conversation, we feel that he is simply describing an objective situation in objective terms and that the allusive or metaphoric dimension of his language reflects the impression Johnson invariably makes on those who come in contact with him. Such language is not reserved for purely comic scenes; consider an incident that occurs when Johnson is talking to some young ladies about Christian friendship:

> From this pleasing subject, he, I know not how or why, made
> a sudden transition to one upon which he was a violent ag-

gressor; for he said, 'I am willing to love all mankind, *except an American:* 'and his inflammable corruption bursting into horrid fire, he 'breathed out threatenings and slaughter;' calling them, 'Rascals—Robbers—Pirates;' and exclaiming, he'd 'burn and destroy them.' Miss Seward, looking at him with mild but steady astonishment, said, 'Sir, this is an instance that we are always most violent against those whom we have injured.'—He was irritated still more by this delicate and keen reproach; and roared out another tremendous volley which one might fancy could be heard across the Atlantick. (III.290)

There is a kind of comedy in the very abruptness with which Johnson moves from complacence to wrath here, and in the violence of his response to the lady's mild reproach,[5] but Boswell's metaphors ("inflammable corruption," "horrid fire," "tremendous volley") all work to emphasize the real awesomeness of Johnson's anger and draw on a kind of imagery he uses to describe Johnson throughout the *Life:* "notwithstanding occasional explosions of violence, we were all delighted upon the whole with Johnson. I compared him at this time to a warm West-Indian climate, where you have a bright sun, quick vegetation, luxuriant foliage, luscious fruits; but where the same heat sometimes produces thunder, lightening, and earthquakes, in a terrible degree" (III.299–300). This is perhaps as self-conscious as Boswell's description gets, yet even here we feel that the simile reflects the impression of the whole company and has been inspired by the character of the hero.

The effect of Boswell's imagery, in this and a hundred other scenes, is to affirm our perception of Johnson as a character who is larger than life, and to include us among those who acknowledge his superiority. Even in the most intimate scenes of the *Life*, Boswell's language reminds us of the distance that lies between Johnson and ordinary men and dramatizes a quality of greatness that is fully revealed only in the personality of the hero. There is more to Johnson's greatness than his moral and intellectual superiority, of course, but in the *Life* the two are related in much the same way as they are in formal tragedy, giving us a protagonist whose largeness of soul fits him for a kind of heroic suffering unknown to the rest of mankind.

THREE

There are a number of scenes in the *Life of Johnson* where Boswell, with a caricaturist's sense of gesture as meaning, catches his hero in a posture that reveals some hidden trait of mind or character. These are, in fact, the scenes from which the nineteenth century derived its view of Johnson as a great eccentric, and though that view (like much that was touched by Lord Macaulay) is itself a caricature, the scenes do exist, and a minor but important theme of the *Life* concerns Johnson's odd behavior. For in one aspect Boswell's portrayal of his hero belongs to the venerable tradition of the "humor," and Johnson as an eccentric is in a literary company that includes Falstaff, Sir Roger de Coverley, Sterne's Uncle Toby, Fielding's Parson Adams, and a hundred characters in Dickens.

Yet the humor type in comic drama and fiction is an obsessive character whose self-absorption fits him awkwardly for the real world, and Johnson's occasional oddities scarcely make him that: only in isolated moments of eccentricity does he exhibit a similar kind of behavior, reminding us that for all his greatness he has never learned that "consistency of appearance" that the world has agreed to call normalcy. This is what Boswell has in mind when, having observed that "man is, in general, made up of contradictory qualities; and these will ever shew themselves in strange succession," he goes on to speak of Johnson: "at different times, he seemed a different man, in some respects; not, however, in any great or essential article, upon which he had fully employed his mind, and settled certain principles of duty, but only in his manners, and in the display of argument and fancy in his talk" (IV.426).

Though Boswell is here using the word *manners* in an almost modern sense, it still suggests something of the preoccupation with social forms that gave the word its large eighteenth-century meaning. Especially in light of Johnson's character as hero, for Johnson conceives of himself as a man who is highly attentive to matters of form, and he argues consistently in the *Life* that a reverence for forms is inseparable from a reverence for the social order. There is a kind of bustle about Johnson's attention to behavior which shows how important he considers the concept: deference to a nobleman becomes, for instance, deference to the great principle of subordination, or respect shown to a clergyman a sign of respect for religion. As a notion governing social behavior, we should guess that this leaves little room for singularity; a man who forms his outward actions according to the ideas of orthodoxy and tradition will find himself in accord with the wiser part of society, and there is little motive for eccentricity.

Seen against this background of meticulous attention to social manners, Johnson's moments of odd behavior reveal the precise degree to which the real relation of the hero to his society in the *Life* is disharmonious. For Johnson appears in the *Life* as a figure who lives in the private world of his own orthodoxy, who devotes much of his time to defending society and its norms from their attackers, and who seems never to notice that his orthodoxy and that of society are seldom the same. Johnson's odd behavior in the *Life* is in fact a type of complete social obliviousness; consider Boswell's famous description of Johnson at table: "he was totally absorbed in the business of the moment; his looks seemed rivetted to his plate; nor would he . . . say one word, or even pay the least attention to what was said by others, till he had satisfied his appetite, which was so fierce, and indulged with such intenseness, that while in the act of eating, the veins on his forehead swelled" (I.468).

Johnson's behavior here goes beyond eccentricity, but only in degree, for Boswell's description catches his hero in precisely the kind of obsessive posture we expect from someone whose existence is ruled by a tendency to complete self-absorption. It reminds us of all those scenes in the *Life* which show Johnson withdrawing into himself, standing alone at one end of a room filled with people, muttering under his breath, reading a book that someone has left out, or just staring out a window. At such moments Johnson's behavior is merely strange; it becomes comic only when his obliviousness is less complete, as in another well-known passage where Boswell describes "his anxious care to go out or in at a door or passage, by a certain number of steps from a certain point": "I have, upon innumerable occasions, observed him suddenly stop, and then seem to count his steps with a deep earnestness; and when he had neglected or gone wrong in this sort of magical movement, I have seen him go back again, put himself in a proper posture to begin the ceremony, and, having gone through it, break from his abstraction, walk briskly on, and join his companion" (I.484–85).

When Johnson's self-absorption is controlled and momentary, as here, we move closer to the conventional idea of comic eccentricity. Yet the difference between Johnson's indulgence of this superstitious habit and his behavior at table is only relative, and we see both against a larger pattern in his existence. For the *Life* shows Johnson, at one extreme, living in a private and separate world: this is the mental state in which Johnson, when he is alone, is most susceptible to melancholy and despair, and the social behavior that corresponds to it is often rude and disturbing. At the other extreme, we see Johnson totally immersed in company and conversation, a situation in which he has managed temporarily to escape the workings of his own morbid fancy and in which society becomes a refuge from the private self.

The scenes in the *Life* which deal with Johnson's odd behavior, and which usually portray some comic moment of minor eccentricity, come when the hero is at a point between the two extremes, neither totally self-involved nor yet totally aware of the situation. The comedy is invariably in the anomalous balance he manages to strike between the two. Here is Beauclerk's account of Johnson's meeting with Madame de Boufflers:

> When our visit was over, she and I left him, and were got into Inner Temple-lane, when all at once I heard a noise like thunder. This was occasioned by Johnson, who it seems, upon a little recollection, had taken into his head that he ought to have done the honours of his literary residence to a foreign lady of quality, and eager to show himself a man of gallantry, was hurrying down the staircase in violent agitation. He overtook us before we reached the Temple-gate, and brushing in between me and Madame de Boufflers, seized her hand, and conducted her to her coach. His dress was a rusty brown morning suit, a pair of old shoes by way of slippers, a little shrivelled wig sticking on the top of his head, and the sleeves of his shirt and the knees of his breeches hanging loose. A considerable crowd of people gathered round, and were not a little struck by this singular appearance. (II.405–6)

Finally, the scenes concerning Johnson's eccentricity deal with a mental state, for in them Boswell catches Johnson in a moment of disequilibrium where we are able to glimpse, just for an instant, what normally goes on in Johnson's private world. Vladimir Nabokov, with his delicate sense of the ludicrous, has made one of these more famous than all the rest; it concerns Johnson's cat Hodge, "for whom he himself used to go out and buy oysters, lest the servants, having that trouble, should take a dislike to the poor creature": "this reminds me of the ludicrous account which he gave Mr. Langton, of the despicable state of a young Gentleman of good family. 'Sir, when I heard of him last, he was running about town shooting cats.' And then in a sort of kindly reverie, he bethought himself of his own favourite cat, and said, 'But Hodge shan't be shot: no, no, Hodge shall not be shot'" (IV.197).

This is, as everyone knows, the passage which Nabokov chose

as the epigraph to *Pale Fire*. In it he saw, one supposes, an emblem of what has become his favorite theme; for Johnson's eccentricity, even as it symbolizes a kind of comic isolation from his society, has a necessary relationship to the darker and more tragic aspects of his existence. Johnson's occasional oddities are not odd merely, for through them we understand that there is something at once comic and tragic about the fact that every man lives in a private world of the imagination, a world of doubts and fears and fantasies which have, on examination, very little to do with what is called reality, but from which there is no escape.

FOUR

Related to Johnson's eccentricity is the contradiction, so often mentioned in the *Life*, between the roughness of his manner and his actual good-heartedness. The Johnson of the *Life* is, with such figures as Smollett's Matthew Bramble, a peculiarly eighteenth-century version of the reliable stereotype, the crusty old gentleman with a heart of gold. This character is so traditional as to seem to belong as much to folklore as to literature, but in the eighteenth century it takes on a coloring from benevolist ethical theory, or at least from the watered-down version of that theory which is embodied in the "sentimental" literature of the period. Boswell's portrayal of Johnson lies in this respect somewhere between Shaftesbury's *Characteristicks* and the benevolist characters of Dickens (especially such rough specimens as Lawrence Boythorn in *Bleak House* and Mr. Grimwig in *Oliver Twist*).

For an author, the benevolist character presents a peculiar problem: if he is seen as being purely benevolent, innocent of any normal human failings and even of any vigorous assertion of personality, he becomes faceless and insipid—one thinks of Squire Alworthy or Dickens's Cheeryble brothers. There are a number of solutions to the problem, but all ultimately involve the notion of showing benevolence as a submerged impulse, one which takes on its value through contrast with contrary traits of character. When the disguise is nearly transparent, as in Goldsmith's *Vicar of Wakefield* or the numbers of the *Spectator* which deal with Sir Roger de Coverley, we are still fairly close to the norm of the sentimental story. The *Life of Johnson*, with a hero whose real generosity of soul is often completely hidden by the roughness of his manner, is at the opposite extreme.

Yet even while Johnson's irascibility solves one problem for Boswell, it creates another: when benevolence is so effectively disguised by brusqueness, how can it be shown to exist at all? Especially when so much of the *Life* deals with conversation, which Johnson always treats as a serious contest, showing little regard for the feelings of his opponents while the dispute is on and resorting repeatedly to ad hominem attack when he feels he is in danger of losing a point. Boswell's effort is to show that the people closest to Johnson, who understand the fierce nature of his intellectual pride, take his manner in conversation as a special case: "let me impress upon my readers a just and happy saying of my friend Goldsmith, who knew him well: 'Johnson, to be sure, has a roughness in his manner: but no man alive has a more tender heart. *He has nothing of the bear but his skin*' " (II.66); "this little incidental quarrel and reconciliation . . . must be esteemed as one of many proofs which his friends had, that though he might be charged with *bad humour* at times, he was always a *good-natured man*" (II.109).

A second problem, one that points to a tension lying deeper in the *Life*, is the apparent conflict between Johnson's benevolence and his dark and pessimistic view of human nature, which belongs more on the side of Hobbes than of Shaftsbury ("This is worse than Swift," a lady says after one of his more bleak remarks on man in the *Tour to the Hebrides*). Even when he admits the existence of sympathy and compassion as natural human impulses, Johnson insists soberly on their limitations: "BOSWELL. 'I own, Sir, I have not so much feeling for the distress of others, as some people have, or pretend to have. . . .' JOHNSON. 'Sir, it is affectation to pretend to feel the distress of others, as much as they do themselves. It is equally so, as if one should pretend to feel as much pain while a friend's leg is cutting off, as he does' " (II.469).

But then, all through the *Life*, and almost as a separate movement of the narrative, we see Johnson disproving his own contention about human nature. There are Johnson's numerous letters to friends, appealing to them to join him in relieving the distress of yet another poor man; there are the frequent acts of unpremeditated charity; there is Johnson's household full of impoverished dependents—Mr. Levet, Mrs. Williams, Mrs. Desmoulins—all portraying a side of Johnson's existence that is almost a continual exercise in benevolence. And beyond this is the instinctive humanity Johnson displays in ordinary situations; Boswell describes his chance meeting with an old schoolfellow who has turned out a failure, "a low man, dull and untaught" and in the first stages of alcoholism: "he had tried to be a cutler at Birmingham, but had not succeeded; and now he lived poorly at home, and had some scheme of dressing leather in a better manner than common; to his indistinct account of which, Dr. Johnson listened with patient attention" (II.463). The scene, as Boswell observes, is one of genuine humanity and real kindness, and it is thoroughly typical of Johnson: "a thousand such instances might have been recorded in the course of his long life."

The paradox of a benevolist hero who argues against all theories of benevolence, and in fact against every suggestion of the idea that virtue is natural to man, is resolved only in the context of Johnson's spiritual struggle. For Johnson's bleak view of human nature is inseparable from his will to discover meaning in human suffering; and, though we often hear in his voice the solemn tones of the preacher reminding a worldly congregation about the Fall of Man, it is something that goes beyond his attachment to orthodox Christian doctrine. The inner reality of human existence is for him a conflict of good and evil, or virtue and vice, and the conflict has no meaning unless one perceives man as a creature who carries the warring opposites within his own nature. Theories of natural virtue are mistaken because they deny the reality of this inward struggle, and pernicious because they rob suffering of its dignity.

Here, once again, we are dealing with Johnson's usual impulse to universalize his own experience, for the ultimate failure of benevolism as a doctrine is its inability to explain his sense of inward conflict. Yet this tendency to turn inward to find the answer to moral questions is precisely the one that governs Johnson's life of active benevolence: the same process of self-examination which reveals innate virtue to be an illusion assures one that outward distress is genuine, and becomes a principle of sympathy. In the end the *Life* suggests that Johnson's superficial roughness of manner and his deeper generosity of soul derive equally from the conviction that human existence is synonymous with human suffering. The suggestion is present throughout the *Life,* but it emerges most strongly in Johnson's last years, where we have a picture of the hero, patient and enduring, living in a house full of quarreling dependents who look to his narrow pension for their support, holding steadfastly to the view that human beings are not, by nature, benevolent.

FIVE

One of the ways in which Boswell associates Johnson with an idealized past is to portray him as a man whose learning is inseparable from his greatness and whose deep commitment to an older tradition of humanistic knowledge already marks him as something of an anachronism. For in an age when the dynamic

classicism of the Renaissance has begun finally to fail, when scholarship has degenerated into narrow pedantry and literature and
philosophy are daily seeking out new and unfamiliar forms of
expression, Johnson's learning retains a special character—"not
backward and trivial, but deep, accurate, ancient, Latin and
Greek." The phrase, which occurs in Erasmus's account of the
learned men (Colet, Linacre, More) he met on his first visit to
England in the late fifteenth century, embraces a humanist conception which identifies classical learning with moral vision. This
is the meaning of Johnson's learning in the *Life*.

Johnson's learning is seen in the *Life* not simply as an enormous
intellectual achievement, though it is that too, but as an attribute
of self, a shaping principle of perception that draws the mind
instinctively toward the permanent and universal component of
human experience. For if Johnson's wide and various reading, as
it ranges eclectically from Virgil and Livy to some modern work
on political economy or improved agricultural methods, seems
inspired by the unsystematic curiosity we associate with the Enlightenment, his basic attitudes derive consistently from a classical perspective on man and society. Johnson's forays into the
world of modern ideas are part of his problematic engagement
with the present, but behind them lies a fundamental assurance
that while the world in one aspect is always changing, it remains
in a deeper sense the same.

In associating Johnson's learning with the universality of his
moral vision, moreover, Boswell is circumventing any tendency
to see Johnson merely as a neoclassical holdout, a survivor of the
age of Swift and Pope who has somehow lingered on into the
later years of the eighteenth century. For that view, while it is
obviously too narrow to satisfy Boswell's large conception of
Johnson as hero, is also inappropriate to his perception of the
present age: the *Life* accepts it in principle that the battle between the Ancients and the Moderns was a rearguard action, and
that the Moderns in the end have won the war. This is why Bos-

well's portrayal of Johnson as a scholar living in the world recalls an earlier age, a time when kings and queens wrote Greek and Latin and the learned man was a considerable figure in society, and it is ultimately why the *Life* is able to locate Johnson in an ethical tradition that reaches back through the Renaissance humanism to the philosopher-hero of antiquity.

In this public and symbolic aspect, Johnson's learning belongs to the story of his conflict with the radically antitraditional tendencies of his own age. At the same time, however, Johnson's lifelong commitment to serious study appears as a major theme in the drama of his private struggle against despair, for as an activity of the rational intellect, learning is a metaphor for consciousness itself: " 'he used to quote, with great warmth,' " reports Langton in the *Life*, " 'the saying of Aristotle recorded by Diogenes Laertius; that there was the same difference between one learned and unlearned, as between the living and the dead' " (IV.13). If Aristotle's remark can be taken to refer to a *state* of consciousness—as in part it should be—it also refers to a process, for while life is simply bestowed, learning must be painfully earned, and for just this reason becomes an affirmation of the rational self.

The story of Johnson's intellectual development is in this sense the story of his growth as a moral hero. As a young man, already a precocious scholar, Johnson displays a curiosity which has almost the status of an ethical yearning; one of Boswell's anecdotes describes him climbing to an upper shelf of his father's bookshop to look for some apples which he imagines to be hidden behind a large folio: "there were no apples; but the large folio proved to be Petrarch, whom he had seen mentioned, in some preface, as one of the restorers of learning. His curiosity having been thus excited, he sat down with avidity, and read a great part of the book. What he read during those two years, he told me, was not works of mere amusement, 'not voyages and travels, but all literature, Sir, all ancient writers, all manly' " (I.57). The anecdote is almost a parable of the mind's discovery of itself.

The meaning of the parable lies in the spontaneity of Johnson's response, for in the acquisition of formal knowledge the young Johnson is as dilatory as the older Johnson will be about his writing: there is early evidence of a powerful and retentive intellect, and there are occasional performances that promise future brilliance, but Johnson's years in school portend his lifelong dislike of steady application. Yet all during his youth he reads continuously, and we are always aware of the sense in which learning as an instinctive pursuit mirrors his process of self-development. Throughout the *Life* Johnson will speak consistently in favor of rigor and discipline in the classroom and will then insist, with equal warmth, that young men should read just as inclination leads them. There is no contradiction: a schoolmaster's whipping is justified if it impels an unwilling youth to learn the declension of *puella*, but only spontaneous curiosity will lead him to the Petrarch on the upper shelf.

The impulse behind Johnson's early reading thus belongs to a larger entelechy of the self, and his pure delight in learning is really an exhilarating awareness of growth in consciousness. Yet this process contains a sad eventual irony, for growth in consciousness involves an inevitable discovery of the pain which accompanies every human activity. The moment of this discovery, in a man of Johnson's nature, marks the onset of maturity, which is the end not only of psychological innocence but of intellectual spontaneity. A year before his death, we hear Johnson speaking of reading in this somber light: "people in general do not willingly read, if they can have anything else to amuse them. There must be an external impulse; emulation, or vanity, or avarice. The progress which the mind makes through a book, has more pain than pleasure in it" (IV.218).

Still, through his middle years and on into old age, Johnson continues not simply to read but to read continuously and systematically, as in a program of formal study. His remark about the pain of reading is followed by this admission: "however, I have this year read all Virgil through. I read a book of the Aeneid every night, so it was done in twelve nights, and I had great delight in it. The Georgicks did not give me so much pleasure, except the fourth book. The Eclogues I have almost by heart." The motive behind such reading is not emulation or vanity or avarice but Johnson's implicit conviction that self-complacence, in a man whose learning is already considerable, represents a kind of spiritual surrender. At a certain point we begin to understand Johnson's unwavering dedication to formal learning, which survives even his worst periods of lethargy and despair, as obedience to an inner imperative that identifies intellectual with moral growth.

As a process, therefore, Johnson's learning belongs almost wholly to the tragic drama of his private struggle against hopelessness. As with his melancholy, this is something we see most clearly in the *Prayers and Meditations*, where learning appears again and again as a spiritual concern: " 'between Easter and Whitsuntide, having always considered that time as propitious to study, I attempted to learn the Low Dutch language' " (II.263); " 'I have retired hither, to plan a life of greater diligence, in hope that I may yet be useful, and be daily better prepared to appear before my Creator and my Judge. . . . Having prayed, I purpose to employ the next six weeks upon the Italian language, for my settled study' " (IV.134–35); " 'O GOD, who hast ordained that whatever is to be desired should be sought by labour . . . look with mercy upon my studies. . . .' This was composed when he 'purposed to apply vigorously to study, particularly of the Greek and Italian tongues' " (II.90).

In the *Prayers and Meditations* Johnson's devotion to serious study appears most often in a penitential light, as something associated not merely with spiritual discipline but with a symbolic renunciation of the world. But beneath this religious concern lies a significance that is really existential, for when one believes deeply that the life of a man is the life of the mind, a prayer for intellectual strength and purpose is a prayer, quite simply, for life itself. Throughout the middle years the existential meaning of Johnson's concern with learning is largely implied, but toward the end, when it merges with his growing horror of death, the theme becomes explicit: "in the latter part of his life, in order to satisfy himself whether his mental faculties were impaired, he resolved that he would try to learn a new language, and fixed upon the Low Dutch, for that purpose, and this he continued till he had read about one half of 'Thomas à Kempis'; and finding that there appeared no abatement of his power of acquisition, he then desisted" (IV.21); "we talked of old age. Johnson (now in his seventieth year,) said, 'It is a man's own fault, it is from want of use, if his mind grows torpid in old age.' . . . One of the company rashly observed, that he thought it was happy for an old man that insensibility comes upon him. JOHNSON: (with a noble elevation and disdain,) 'No, Sir, I should never be happy by being less rational' " (III.254–55).

Only during the gathering spiritual anxiety of Johnson's final years, perhaps, is his lifelong devotion to learning wholly revealed as an aspect of his isolation from the present age. In a sense the theme has been present throughout the *Life*, for Johnson's conflict with the antiintellectual tendencies of the Enlightenment has ranged from the most ordinary matters—"JOHNSON. 'Nay, Sir, how can you talk so? What is *climate* to happiness?' " (II.195)—to those which spring directly from the new primitivism of Rousseau and his followers:

> a learned gentleman . . . expatiated on the happiness of a savage life, and mentioned an instance of an officer who had actually lived for some time in the wilds of America, of whom, when in that state, he quoted this reflection with an air of admiration, as if it had been deeply philosophical: 'Here am I, free and unrestrained, amidst the rude magnificence of Nature, with this Indian woman by my side, and this gun, with which I can procure food when I want it: what more can be desired for human happiness?' . . . JOHNSON. 'Do not allow yourself, Sir, to be imposed upon by such gross ab-

surdity. It is sad stuff; it is brutish. If a bull could speak, he might as well exclaim,—Here am I with this cow and this grass; what being can enjoy better felicity?' (II.228)

Johnson appears in such scenes as the defender of an older tradition of humanistic learning surrounded on all sides by the antiintellectual doctrines of the philosophes (one thinks of Rousseau's famous boast, in *Émile*, that he hates books). But the conflict runs deeper than that, for Johnson's commitment to learning is in a larger sense only an aspect of his will to believe that there is a meaning in human existence. When Johnson argues against the fashionable doctrine of primitivism, or devotes himself in old age to the learning of a new language, or prays privately for the Lord's blessing upon his studies, he is engaged finally not with notions contrary to his own but with the apparition of a mindless universe in which no human pursuit is higher than another and death means annihilation of the rational self.

In the end, then, the theme of Johnson's learning in the *Life* involves an interplay of public and private meanings; for while it provides, as an accomplishment, symbolic affirmation of Boswell's perception of his hero as a superior being, it belongs as a process to the story of his personal struggle against despair. If on one level we see Johnson in the conventional light of a philosopher-hero in an intellectual world of lesser men and as the last great survivor of a dying tradition of humanistic thought, we see him on another simply as a man whose devotion to the life of the mind springs from a deep instinctive resistance to the notion that human existence is a meaningless drama played out against the backdrop of an eternal necessity without design.

SIX

The major dramatic tension in the *Life*, I have suggested, is between public certainty and private doubt, between the magisterial Johnson who dominates literary London and the deeply disturbed Johnson whose suffering we trace in the *Prayers and Meditations* and letters and personal conversations. This is why nearly every aspect of Johnson's character as hero simultaneously involves a public and a private significance, and why we so often perceive in Johnson's relation to his world a mixture of comedy and tragedy. The single exception is Johnson's melancholy, which belongs as a theme almost wholly to the inward drama of his personal struggle and which more than anything else reveals Boswell's ultimate conception of his hero as a tragic figure.

Johnson's melancholy returns us always to the central problem of the hero isolated from his age, searching for coherence in a world where the orthodox alliance between faith and reason is fast dissolving. Here, once again, we see in Johnson's struggle the beginnings of a spiritual dilemma we normally associate with the nineteenth century; specifically, with the kind of religious despair described by Frederick Robertson: "It is an awful hour— let him who has passed through it say how awful—when this life has lost its meaning, and seems shrivelled into a span; when the grave appears to be the end of all, human goodness nothing but a name, and the sky above this universe a dead expanse, black with the void from which God himself has disappeared."[6]

The *Life,* however, is a story not about despair but about its hero's battle against despair, and the specter of hopelessness Robertson describes appears not as a reality but as a terrifying possibility, something to be resisted with every effort of the mind and will. Yet the growing enmity between faith and reason in the eighteenth-century world of the *Life* has exposed the area of human vulnerability which is the traditional province of tragedy, and it is from the nature of Johnson's resistance that the affinities of the *Life* with formal tragedy derive. "The 'tragic combat,' says Unamuno, the 'very essence of tragedy,' is the 'combat of life with reason.' The 'spirit of submissiveness to death labours to build up the house of life,' while 'the keen blasts and stormy

assaults of reason beat it down.' "[7] Johnson's melancholy, while
it is not tragic in itself, has its origin in this tragic combat and is
(like Lear's madness) an inescapable consequence of his spiritual
isolation.

Yet Johnson cannot, as a hero, admit his isolation, for to do so
would be to lose the struggle against despair. This is why the
story of Johnson's melancholy is so often one of desperate indi-
rection, turning on a basic paradox: on the one hand, Johnson
treats his periods of mental suffering as lapses which somehow
involve a failure of willpower and which can be overcome by a
return to duty and self-discipline. On the other, he allows himself the relief of viewing melancholy as an illness, something
which arrives with the inevitability of consumption or influenza
and is beyond the control of the victim. Or even as an inherited
trait; here is Boswell describing Johnson's father: "there was in
him a mixture of that disease, the nature of which eludes the most
minute enquiry, though the effects are well known to be a weariness of life . . . and a general sensation of gloomy wretchedness.
From him then his son inherited . . . 'a vile melancholy,' which
in his too strong expression of any disturbance of mind 'made
him mad all his life, at least not sober' " (I.35).

In either case Johnson's strategy for dealing with melancholy
is one of avoidance. To treat melancholy as an illness is in a sense
to domesticate it, to view it as the hypochondria or "English
malady" that has exerted something of a cultural fascination at
least since the publication of Burton's *Anatomy* (and in Boswell
we have a narrator strongly disposed toward that view). To treat
hypochondria as a failure of will, on the other hand, is to enter
upon the familiar ground of duty and resolve and to suppose that
what has been caused by lethargy may be cured by exertion.
The single possibility which Johnson refuses categorically to
entertain is that melancholy is neither illness nor failure but the
entirely reasonable retreat of the human spirit from a reality
which is meaningless in human terms. Yet this is just the vision

of reality that haunts Johnson during his periods of gloomy wretchedness and that looms as a dark threat beyond the comfort of conventional explanations.

In this sense, Johnson's hypochondria is a metaphor of spiritual isolation, one that brings us very close to the central symbolic problem of the *Life* and to the nature of Johnson's moral heroism. This is why we perceive melancholy less as a simple theme than as a principle that gives shape to the story as a whole and that allows us continuously to glimpse the tragic meaning even of the conversational scenes, ordinarily so full of life and comedy. Again and again Boswell recalls us to a sobering awareness of the suffering that underlies Johnson's social exuberance: "while his friends in their intercourse with him constantly found a vigorous intellect and a lively imagination, it is melancholy to read in his private register, 'My mind is unsettled and my memory confused. . . . I have yet got no command over my thoughts; an unpleasing incident is almost certain to hinder my rest'" (II.190); "it was observed to Dr. Johnson, that it seemed strange that he, who has so often delighted his company by his lively and brilliant conversation, should say he was miserable. JOHNSON. 'Alas! it is all outside; I may be cracking my joke, and cursing the sun. *Sun, how I hate thy beams!*'" (IV.304).

In any scene that shows Johnson in a state of lively animation, we are aware of the temporary compromise with despair that underlies his momentary exuberance. Thus, even when Johnson seems totally absorbed in the external situation, the darker reality of his personal suffering is apt to show through in unexpected ways. This is why Joshua Reynolds, for instance, explains Johnson's famous convulsions as involuntary actions "'meant to reprobate some part of his past conduct. Whenever he was not engaged in conversation, such thoughts were sure to rush into his mind; and, for this reason, any company, any employment whatever, he preferred to being alone'" (I.144). Boswell duly records the more conventional opinion that Johnson's convulsions were caused by some physical disorder like epilepsy or St. Vitus's Dance, but it is Reynolds who speaks to the symbolic truth of the situation, and in whose explanation we see the larger dilemma of the hero.

The great conversation scenes of the *Life*, therefore, while they have their own meaning as intellectual drama and often as social comedy, take their final meaning from their relationship to Johnson's inward conflict; as Reynolds notes at the end of his remarks, " 'the great business of his life (he said) was to escape from himself; this disposition he considered as the disease of his mind, which nothing cured but company.' " The *Life* most often shows Johnson in company, and the comic vitality of Boswell's finest scenes usually depends on an active assortment of characters surrounding the hero, but once we perceive these same scenes as episodes in Johnson's constant struggle to escape from himself, we cannot help but be aware of the shadow of tragic implication that lies across them. In a sense the parts of the *Life* that seem to have the least to do with Johnson's spiritual isolation are those that concern it most directly.

Once Boswell has described the desperate motivation behind Johnson's excursions into society, he is content to focus on Johnson's actual behavior in company and conversation and to remind us only occasionally of the deeper meaning of the familiar picture of Johnson holding forth in tavern or drawing room. Yet we are always aware that we are ultimately watching a drama of spiritual survival and that company and conversation are fragile barricades to set against despair; when they crumble, the apparition of hopelessness is suddenly revealed: "he was so ill, as, notwithstanding his remarkable love of company, to be entirely averse to society. . . . Dr. Adams told me . . . that he found him in a deplorable state, sighing, groaning, talking to himself, and restlessly walking from room to room. He then used this emphatical expression of the misery which he felt: 'I would consent to have a limb amputated to recover my spirits' " (I.483).

Still, the scenes in the *Life* that actually show Johnson's mental suffering are comparatively few, and the idea of melancholy runs as a submerged theme through the larger story. More often we are reminded of its presence by Johnson himself, in his public role as moralist and sage. Johnson's tendency to universalize his own experience is nowhere more apparent than in the bleak view of human existence which characterizes the highest reaches of his moral thought, a view which derives immediately from his own sense of personal misery: "he asserted, that *the present* was never a happy state to any human being. . . . and asked if he really was of the opinion, that though, in general, happiness was very rare in human life, a man was not sometimes happy in the moment that was present, he answered, 'Never, but when he is drunk'" (II.350–51). In this sense Johnson's melancholy lies at the heart of the classical and Christian attitudes that so govern his antagonism toward the present age.

At the same time, and largely because it springs so immediately from his sense of personal misery, Johnson's gloomy view of human existence defines the nature of his heroism. As a metaphor of isolation, melancholy represents the paralysis of the mind confronted with a universe vacant of meaning, and the struggle against melancholy is symbolically the purest form of resistance to the idea. This is why Johnson, even as he insists in the bleakest terms that the pursuit of earthly happiness is futile and delusive, is able to maintain without paradox that activity has meaning nonetheless: "when I, in a low-spirited fit, was talking to him with indifference of the pursuits which generally engage us in a course of action, and enquiring a *reason* for taking so much trouble; 'Sir, (said he, in an animated tone) it is driving on the system of life'" (IV.112).

Nothing else in the *Life*, perhaps, better epitomizes the spirit of "philosophick heroism" which Boswell took as the essence of Johnson's moral greatness. As an attitude distilled from personal suffering, this is a heroism that, even as it takes ordinary life as its proper sphere, transforms commonplace events into a drama of higher significance. If there is already a tragic implication in the picture of Johnson appearing with "manly fortitude to the world" while he is "inwardly so distressed," there is a more inclusive notion of heroic purpose involved in his undertaking any activity at all—an excursion to Vauxhall or an evening party at Streatham as much as the compilation of the *Dictionary* or the writing of the *Lives of the Poets*.

At the beginning of the *Life* Boswell describes his mode of biography as one that will allow us to " 'live o'er each scene' " with Johnson "as he actually advanced through the several stages of his life" (I.30). The phrase, which is from Pope's prologue to Addison's *Cato*, reminds us not only that the *Life* is in the traditional sense a story about a hero but that Boswell is conscious of dealing with a conventional theme in an unconventional context. Because the concept of philosophic heroism surrounds everyday scenes with heroic implication, and ultimately transforms the eighteenth-century world of the *Life* into a heroic setting, we are able to perceive in Johnson's existence the spectacle (to borrow another line from Pope's prologue) of "a brave man struggling in the storms of fate" even as we recognize the unheroic nature of the society around him.

In the *Life* Boswell's concern with the figure of the hero in an unheroic world thus leads inevitably to an emphasis on the sense in which Johnson's existence has emerged from a compromise with despair. In the middle years we most often glimpse Johnson's sense of isolation in his letters: " 'I hope, in a few days, to be at leisure, and to make visits. Whither I shall fly is matter of no importance. A man unconnected is at home every where; unless he may be said to be at home no where' " (I.347); " 'I was glad to go abroad, and, perhaps, glad to come home . . . in other words, I was, I am afraid, weary of being at home, and weary of being abroad. Is not this the state of life?' " (II.382). In such remarks, where we normally hear Johnson addressing some sympathetic friend, we perceive the troubled reality that lies behind the positive pronouncements of the moralist in his public role.

For similar reasons the *Prayers and Meditations* become increasingly important in Johnson's later years, when his melancholy begins to merge with his growing horror of death. If Johnson's familiar correspondence allows some degree of private revelation, the *Prayers and Meditations* demand it, and carry us to the heart of his personal conflict. As Boswell reminds us from time to time, these are thoughts written "in the genuine earnestness of secrecy" and in full consciousness of a divine and omniscient audience; in them the theme of tragic isolation emerges as a barely-suppressed cry for help: " 'when I survey my past life, I discover nothing but a barren waste of time, with some disorders of body, and disturbances of mind, very near to madness, which I hope He that made me will suffer to extenuate many faults' " (III.99); " 'have mercy upon me, o GOD, have mercy upon me; years and infirmities oppress me, terrour and anxiety beset me. Have mercy upon me, my Creator and my Judge' " (III.99).

Johnson's great struggle is to see his isolation in orthodox Christian terms and to explain his misery as a radical uncertainty about his own salvation. In this sense he is addressing the *deus absconditus* of Pascal's *Pensées*, and his sense of human suffering as a condition of man's divided nature is superficially similar. But the resemblance is only superficial, for in Pascal we have someone for whom the grand synthesis of medieval Christianity is still a source of spiritual strength and for whom the sceptical relativism of writers like Montaigne does not yet pose an ultimate threat. But in the eighteenth-century world of the *Life*, where the Augustinian synthesis is a remote curiosity of intellectual history and where the mild relativism of Montaigne has given place to the powerful and menacing scepticism of Hume, the confidence in universal order that sustained Pascal has all but disappeared.

Still, even in his deepest moments of personal misery, Johnson never abandons the struggle to channel his despair into orthodox doubts. Thus we have, all through the *Life,* conversations in which religious sceptics like Hume are dismissed out of hand and other conversations in which the company is allowed to see Johnson's open concern for salvation: "MRS. ADAMS. 'You seem, Sir, to forget the merits of our Redeemer.' JOHNSON. 'Madam, I do not forget the merits of my Redeemer; but my Redeemer has said that he will set some on his right hand and some on his left.'—He was in gloomy agitation, and said, 'I'll have no more on't'" (IV.300). Beneath the passionate sincerity of his doubts about salvation, however, we sense the precariousness of Johnson's orthodoxy. Thus we have, on the one hand, the Johnson who listens eagerly to any story about the supernatural, ghosts and mysterious voices being (whatever the cost to rational scepticism) one proof that the soul is immortal. On the other, we have the Johnson who gazes longingly toward the comforting certainty of Roman Catholic doctrine or who carefully hedges his own orthodoxy, as when he avows a conditional belief in the efficacy of prayers for the dead, or who impulsively strikes out in some act that symbolizes both his uncertainty and his hope: "'once, indeed, (said he,) I was disobedient; I refused to attend my father to Uttoxeter-market. . . . A few years ago I desired to atone for this fault. I went to Uttoxeter in very bad weather, and stood for a considerable time bareheaded in the rain, on the spot where my father's stall used to stand. In contrition I stood, and I hope the penance was expiatory'" (IV.373).

If Johnson anticipates the tendency of nineteenth-century intellectuals to seek refuge from religious despair in Catholicism, he appears in the *Life* as a great man because his response is not the same as theirs. Johnson is an isolated figure because he clairvoyantly recognizes in his own age the invisible forces that will later lead to a general breakdown in faith, and he is a moral hero because he confronts them with a brave orthodoxy sustained largely by his own mind and will. Yet this process necessarily involves a kind of spiritual attrition, and in some final sense we come to see Johnson's melancholy as a weariness of the soul tired out in the tragic combat of life with reason. " 'A man may have such a degree of hope as to keep him quiet,' " Johnson says at one point. " 'You see I am not quiet, from the vehemence with which I talk; but I do not despair' " (IV.299–300).

The theme of melancholy in the *Life* leads us ultimately to a conception of the hero that looks both backward and forward in time. As a Christian hero in an age of growing doubt, Johnson is associated with an idealized past in which faith and reason were one and with an idea of universal coherence that runs back through Augustine to Aristotle. But as an isolated figure in a society which does not perceive the imminence of its own spiritual disintegration and which understands his misery only as a kind of moral eccentricity, Johnson resembles the alienated hero of postromantic mythology. In a story set in the unheroic world of eighteenth-century England, this isolation has a special significance: the argument of the *Life*, if we can borrow that word from its epic context, is that the realm of heroic conflict, like the kingdom of Heaven, is within us.

SEVEN

Through the greater part of the *Life* the tragic and comic elements of Johnson's story are mixed, for as a hero in an unheroic world, Johnson inhabits the sort of milieu conventionally associated with comedy. Thus it often happens that the very qualities that at certain times affirm our sense of Johnson's suffering or of his superiority to other men—his learning, his benevolence, his eccentricity—at others figure largely in the comedy of manners that occupies the foreground of the narrative. Even the subject of Johnson's melancholy, now and again allowing us a glimpse into the darker world of inward struggle that lies behind the comedy, is only an occasional theme, one which regularly gives way to the crowded conviviality of the conversation scenes. The *Life* is a book that (in Boswell's phrase) embraces "the strangely mixed scenes of human existence" in all their variety, and that shows the gaiety of Johnson's life along with its sadness.

Yet during the last part of the *Life*, beginning with Johnson's decline and ending with his death, the mood of the story inexorably darkens. There are still moments of comedy, but now they occur in a dramatic context that has grown steadily more serious. This is the part of the *Life* that deals with the passing of the hero, and in it we discover, as in the final movement of a symphony, both a restatement and a resolution of the major themes we have pursued throughout the whole. In the story of Johnson's dying we have, on the one hand, the conventional and reassuring image of the Christian hero passing to his reward "perfectly composed, steady in hope, and resigned to death," and, on the other, the equally conventional and no less moving image of the passing of the philosopher-hero.

To speak of these images as being conventional is to invoke once again the notion of conventions as the symbolic and dramatic principles governing literary works. For though Boswell's account of his hero's confrontation with death draws on the conventions of earlier narrative, the final meaning of Johnson's passing is anything but conventional in the more ordinary sense. In this final portion of the *Life* we are dealing in a heightened and ultimate sense with the major theme of Boswellian narrative, the theme of the genuine hero existing in an unheroic age. The death of Johnson is not merely the death of a great and good man but the final disappearance of heroic potentiality from a world alien to heroism.

To perceive the sense in which Johnson's death as a Christian hero represents a continuation and a fulfillment of Boswell's major theme, there must be present to our minds the long and complex story of Johnson's struggle throughout the *Life* as a whole, a struggle to work out his spiritual destiny within the confines of Christian orthodoxy—within the comprehensible and finally ennobling context of Christ's propitiatory sacrifice and the possibility of eternal salvation—in a world increasingly dominated by the clamor of scepticism, materialism, and unbelief. Almost from the beginning of the narrative we are aware of Johnson's heroism as a power, won through an enormous exercise of mind and will, to shut the clamor out: "I told him that David Hume said to me, he was no more uneasy to think he should *not be* after this life, than that he *had not been* before he began to exist. JOHNSON. 'Sir, if he really thinks so, his perceptions are disturbed; he is mad; if he does not think so, he lies. He may tell you, he holds his finger in the flame of a candle, without feeling pain; would you believe him? When he dies, he at least gives up all he has' " (II.106).

The terror lurking in Hume's cheerful resignation is the terror of death as annihilation, the extinction of rational consciousness against the background of the universe as a blank and meaningless waste. This is the context in which a belief in Christian salvation, even as it entails a corollary belief in the possibility of eternal damnation, represents a victory over utter meaninglessness: "MISS SEWARD. 'There is one mode of the fear of death, which is certainly absurd; and that is the dread of annihilation, which is only a pleasing sleep without a dream.' JOHNSON. 'It is neither pleasing, nor sleep; it is nothing. Now mere existence is so much better than nothing, that one would rather exist even in pain, than not exist' " (III.295–96). And this too is the context in which Johnson's religious struggle assumes a simultaneous existential significance; for death, as Wittgenstein reminds us, is not an event we live to experience. It is comprehensible only as a problem—in the *Life*, the central problem—of existence itself: "JOHNSON. 'The lady confounds annihilation, which is nothing, with the apprehension of it, which is dreadful. It is in the

apprehension of it that the horrour of annihilation consists' "
(III.296).

Through the last scenes of the *Life*, then, our perception of
Johnson as Christian hero is enlarged and complicated by an
awareness that we are witnessing the end of an existential drama.
The *Life* portrays Johnson as a hero not merely because he was
a Christian—its pages are filled with figures, from John Wesley
to the devout Mrs. Knowles, whose Christian faith is unperturbed
by the onslaught of the philosophes—but because his orthodoxy
represents a triumph of mind and spirit in an age of growing unbelief. This is the final meaning of the reassurance Boswell discovers in Johnson's presence: "I complained of a wretched
changefulness, so that I could not preserve, for any long con-
tinuance, the same views of any thing. It was most comfortable
for me to experience, in Dr. Johnson's company, a relief from
this uneasiness. His steady vigorous mind held firm before me
those objects which my own feeble and tremulous imagination
frequently presented, in such a wavering state, that my reason
could not judge well of them" (III.193).

As always in such scenes, Boswell is giving voice to the implicit
principle of community that sustains the inner world of the *Life*,
a world of characters who share a sense of Johnson's "vigorous
reason" as a power of heroic affirmation. Throughout the greater
part of the *Life* this is as true of Johnson's magisterial utterances
on politics and morality and learning as of his pronouncements
on religion, but as his death approaches all else recedes in importance. The image of Johnson as Christian hero embodies, in these
last months, a principle enunciated in a conversation twenty
years before: "As to the Christian religion, Sir, besides the strong
evidence which we have for it, there is a balance in its favour
from the number of great men who have been convinced of its
truth, after a serious consideration of the question. Grotius was
an acute man, a lawyer, a man accustomed to examine evidence,
and he was convinced. . . . Sir Isaac Newton set out an infidel, and

came to be a very firm believer' " (I.454–55). In an age of spiritual dissolution, the strongest evidence for the truth of Christianity is neither theological nor metaphysical; it is the presence among lesser souls of a great man whose inward struggle ends within the boundaries of Christian orthodoxy.

The drama of Johnson's death as a Christian hero remains dramatic precisely because the *Life* insists on the existential dimension of his religious struggle until the last possible moment, throwing into sharp relief themes that have run submerged throughout the earlier story. Throughout the *Life*, for instance, we have listened to Johnson's sympathetic treatment of Roman Catholic doctrine and have heard in his sympathy that longing for ontological certainty that would draw so many nineteenth-century intellectuals, from John Henry Newman to Oscar Wilde, into the embrace of the Church. Now, in the final months, the lure of Roman Catholicism appears as the lure of a retreat from orthodoxy into pure faith, and it is as such that Johnson must resist it: "On the Roman Catholick religion he said, . . . 'There is one side on which a good man might be persuaded to embrace it. A good man, of a timorous disposition, in great doubt of his acceptance with GOD, and pretty credulous, might be glad to be of a church where there are so many helps to get to Heaven. I would be a Papist if I could. I have fear enough; but an obstinate rationality prevents me. I shall never be a Papist, unless on the near approach of death, of which I have a very great terrour' " (IV.289).

In the other direction lies a departure from orthodoxy into doubt—into, in the words of a prayer Johnson composes four months before his death, "unprofitable and dangerous enquiries, . . . difficulties vainly curious, and doubts impossible to be solved" (IV.370). During the final period the victory of mind and spirit that has allowed Johnson to pursue his inward struggle within the bounds of Christian orthodoxy exacts its awful toll in the form of orthodox terror: "The amiable Dr. Adams suggested

that GOD was infinitely good. JOHNSON. 'That he is infinitely
good, as far as the perfection of his nature will allow, I certainly
believe; but it is necessary for good upon the whole, that individuals should be punished. As to an *individual*, therefore, he is not
infinitely good; and as I cannot be *sure* that I have fulfilled the
conditions on which salvation is granted, I am afraid I may be
one of those who shall be damned.' (looking dismally.) DR.
ADAMS. 'What do you mean by damned?' JOHNSON. (passion-
ately and loudly) 'Sent to Hell, Sir, and punished everlastingly' "
(IV.299).

The dramatic context of Johnson's death as a Christian hero,
then, is the total context of his inward struggle through the *Life*
as a whole. The story of that struggle is what prepares us for Boswell's elaborate and detailed account of Johnson's final days and
hours, an account that at last presents us with the conventional
image of the Christian hero who has passed through a torment
of self-doubt and repentance to the tranquility that lies beyond.
It is in this account of Johnson's final composure, of a long death-
bed scene so orchestrated as to seem almost a ritual, that the final
significance of Johnson's religious struggle emerges. His tranquility in his last hours is no longer the private possession of an
heroic spirit but the public possession of the world that survives
him.

Boswell's withdrawal from the scene gives us an early intimation of the public significance of Johnson's death as a steadfast
and resigned Christian, and we are aware that the drama of the
final episode consists not least in its being a public drama. For it
is not simply that this account of Johnson's death is an assemblage
of numerous and various reports but that what occurs within the
episode is a steady procession to the bedside of the dying Christian. There are friends and acquaintances, lawyers and divines,
servants and nurses, and even anonymous characters who appear
for a moment only to disappear forever: "when the service was
ended, he, with great earnestness, turned round to an excellent
lady who was present, saying 'I thank you, Madam, very heartily,

for your kindness in joining me in this solemn exercise. Live well, I conjure you; and you will not feel the compunction at the last, which I now feel' " (IV.410).

The anonymous lady, like the anonymous gentlemen who figure in so many of the great conversation scenes, exists at the outer periphery of the world sustained by Johnson's presence as a moral hero. Like his life as a defender of Christian orthodoxy, Johnson's death as a Christian takes place in the public arena, and his teaching in the last extremity takes the form of an earnest "anxiety for the religious improvement of his friends, to whom he discoursed of its infinite consequences": "Dr. Brocklesby having attended him with the utmost assiduity and kindness as his physician and friend, he was peculiarly desirous that this gentleman should not entertain any loose and speculative notions, but be confirmed in the truths of Christianity, and insisted on his writing down in his presence . . . the import of what passed on the subject: and Dr. Brocklesby having complied with the request, he made him sign the paper, and urged him to keep it in his own custody as long as he lived" (IV.414).

Yet the truth of the image of Johnson as a dying Christian is a wholly conventional truth, for the image is the creation of a world determined to discover in Johnson's manner of dying a source of conventional comfort. This is why, as the narrative portrays Johnson's approach to death more and more in public terms—as it is transformed from a private experience into a cultural memory or myth—the account becomes less and less true to the reality of the *Life* as a whole. The image of Johnson as Christian hero becomes in the last event an order imposed on reality by an age unable to perceive the true nature of his moral heroism. Its public character is revealed once and for all in the fourth-hand relation of Johnson's death, occurring last in the sequence of circumstantial accounts. The account, which has passed from the servant Cawston to the Honorable John Byng to Edmond Malone to Boswell, contains the essence of the Christian hero motif:

It should seem, that Dr. Johnson was perfectly composed, steady in hope, and resigned to death. At the interval of each hour, they assisted him to sit up in his bed, and move his legs, which were in much pain; when he regularly addressed himself to fervent prayer; and though, sometimes, his voice failed him, his senses never did, during that time. The only sustenance he received, was cyder and water. He said his mind was prepared, and the time to his dissolution seemed long. At six in the morning, he enquired the hour, and, on being informed, said that all went on regularly, and he felt he had but a few hours to live.

'At ten o'clock in the morning, he parted from Cawston, saying, "You should not detain Mr. Windham's servant:—I thank you; bear my remembrance to your master." Cawston says, that no man could appear more collected, more devout, or less terrified at the thoughts of the approaching minute. (IV.418–19)

The tension between this image of Johnson as Christian hero and the more disturbing reality of his inward struggle as we have traced it through the earlier story is caught perfectly in the concluding comment of Malone's correspondent: "this account . . . has given us the satisfaction of thinking that that great man died as he lived, full of resignation, strengthened in faith, and joyful in hope." At any suggestion that Johnson lived his life resigned to dying and joyful in hope a hundred scenes crowd into the mind ("'Madam, I do not forget the merits of my Redeemer; but my Redeemer has said that he will set some on his right hand and some on his left.'—He was in gloomy agitation, and said, 'I'll have no more on't' ") to insist on the reality of that deeper and unimaginably more complex image of Johnson created by the *Life* as a whole. The ultimate truth contained in the Christian hero motif is a truth not about Johnson but about his age, which has insisted to the end on seeing both his life and his death in its own terms.

Yet this truth about the age in which Johnson has existed as a beseiged moral hero is no less important a dimension of the *Life*'s meaning than the truth about the real nature of Johnson's heroism, and the very conventionality of the Christian hero motif is in the end an invitation to look beneath the surface of events to a reality consistent with the whole. Throughout the final portion of the *Life*, as a counterpoint to the Christian hero motif, Boswell balances two important themes, the personal and the culturally symbolic, until at the end they converge in the actuality of Johnson's passing. The first of these themes concerns the underlying meaning of the final period as the last spiritual crisis of Johnson's existence, of his ultimate response to the inevitability of death, the event that has horrified him for so many years. The second dwells on the permanent meaning of Johnson's death to his society and age; ultimately, to posterity and the world.

The prelude to Johnson's last illness is his growing sense of isolation as the world he has known passes away and he is left behind. Here Boswell turns again and again to the passages of Johnson's diaries and letters that reveal his deepening recognition that we find the meaning of our life on earth, our sense of identity and even reality, in human relationships. The passing of friends is, in fact, the passing of the world: "I live now but in a melancholy way. My old friend Mr. Levett is dead . . . Mrs. Desmoulins is gone away; and Mrs. Williams is so much decayed, that she can add little to another's gratifications. The world passes away, and we are passing with it' " (IV.233). This is symbolic isolation turned literal: as earlier parts of the *Life* centered on Johnson's escape into company and conversation, this shows him at a time when the hope of such escape is steadily dwindling: " 'I have lost dear Mr. Allen; and wherever I turn, the dead or the dying meet my notice, and force my attention upon misery and mortality' " (IV.360). What remains is a stark confrontation with death.

Seen against the larger background of Johnson's story, this is a confrontation surrounded by an almost archetypal significance, for the *Life* has all along been concerned with that special heroism of mind and spirit we associate with the philosopher-hero. The emotional depth of this last portion of the *Life* derives in large part from Boswell's response to the symbolic problem posed by what might be called the image of the dying philosopher: the notion that the philosopher, as a man possessed of a special vision of life, should confront death in a manner different from that of ordinary men. "It was this ubiquitous preoccupation," explains Peter Gay, "that made Socrates the folk hero of pagan antiquity. Socrates had conquered the problems of life by confronting and defeating death. The story of Socrates' final hours had moved the ancients to heroism as it moved moderns to awe."[8] Behind Boswell's portrayal of the final period of Johnson's life we glimpse a theme as old as Plato's *Phaedo*.

When the dying philosopher is Samuel Johnson, the question of how death is to be faced possesses a special significance. Reflected everywhere in the *Life*, in Johnson's conversation and in the passages of his letters and writings which Boswell makes part of the story, is the gloomy notion that it is the fate of man on earth to live in a continual state of self-deception, imprisoned within an untrustworthy world of fears, hopes, and passions that have little to do with what is external or real. In one aspect it is the contention between this imagined world and the blind, autonomous forces of reality that creates the comedy of human existence: we live to indulge our self-deception and to be brought roughly back to earth, more or less frequently, by the intrusion of an actuality that refuses to operate on our terms. But the approach of death removes the sense of comedy: the actual now appears as the demonic destroyer of poetry and myth, blind and remorseless, reducing all questions of response to utter meaninglessness. Yet one is left, still alive in a world of inescapable self-deception, to find a response.

Over the events of the final period, therefore, there hangs the gloom of Johnson's own intensely pessimistic analysis of human existence and the problem of his answer to an unanswerable question. The event that marks the beginning of this period is Johnson's loss of speech: coming in the night, a mysterious stroke, it is an episode that prefigures death itself; in Johnson's reaction to it, in the unpremeditated stoicism he reveals when he awakens to find himself mute and helpless, we glimpse the inauguration of some final adjustment. Boswell devotes some pages to the episode, but what stands out, poignant and somehow untouched by the note of retrospective accommodation apparent in Boswell's telling of the story, is Johnson's writing to Edmund Allen: "it has pleased GOD, this morning, to deprive me of the powers of speech; and as I do not know but that it may be his further good pleasure to deprive me soon of my senses, I request you will on the receipt of this note, come to me, and act for me, as the exigencies of my case may require' " (IV.228).

From this point on, just as Johnson's symbolic isolation earlier became literal, his spiritual suffering becomes physical, the theme of inevitability asserting itself in the gradual deterioration of the body. We are fastened, said Yeats, to a dying animal; the real terror of the phrase is perhaps obvious only to those who die, not suddenly, but by degrees: " 'having promoted the institution of a new club in the neighbourhood . . . I went thither to meet the company, and was seized with a spasmodick asthma, so violent, that with difficulty I got to my own house, in which I have been confined eight or nine weeks. . . . My nights are very sleepless and very tedious. And yet I am extremely afraid of dying' " (IV.259). The meaning of such scenes, however, lies less in Johnson's terror than in his resolute dedication to human activity in the face of terror. It is the effect of Johnson's behavior during the final period to exalt and at last fix the value of what with him has been a lifelong alternative to despair.

The rhythm of the final months is an alternation of sickness and partial recovery, the former characterized by a desperate helplessness, the latter by Johnson's attempts to throw himself into life with an energy that will crowd despair to the fringes of his consciousness. The worst moments come when Johnson is bedridden and immobile: " 'I would not have the consent of the physician to go to church yesterday. . . . O! my friend, the approach of death is very dreadful. . . . It is vain to look round and round for that help which cannot be had. Yet we hope and hope, and fancy that he who has lived to-day may live to-morrow' " (IV.270). But when Johnson recovers enough to be even partially active, an altogether different spirit asserts itself: "all who saw him, beheld and acknowledged the *invictum animum* Catonis. . . . He said to one friend, 'Sir, I look upon every day to be lost, in which I do not make a new acquaintance;' and to another, when talking of his illness, 'I will be conquered; I will not capitulate' " (IV.374).

In the appearance of this *invictum animum Catonis* we have the final expression of that spirit of "philosophick heroism" that has animated Boswell's portrayal of Johnson from the beginning, and, at the same time, the exposure of a false dilemma. For to reveal in his extremity some special invulnerability to the terror of death, like the philosopher-heroes of antiquity, would be for Johnson to deny the truth of his own bleak analysis of human existence, an analysis inseparable from his character as both philosopher and hero. Yet where there are no solutions there may yet be answers; during these last months one often recalls that earlier exchange between Boswell and Johnson: "when I in a low-spirited fit, was talking to him with indifference of the pursuits which generally engage us in a course of action, and enquiring a reason for taking so much trouble; 'Sir (said he, in an animated tone) it is driving on the system of life' " (IV.112).

It is, Sartre has written, the constant possibility of non-being, outside us and within, that determines the questions we ask and the answers we give to them. Earlier in the *Life* this possibility appeared as the specter, haunting the fringes of Johnson's melancholy, of a blind and meaningless universe; in the final period it takes the form, familiar in tragic and heroic literature, of death.

But Johnson's response, one which makes his heroism all of a whole, has in both cases been the same: to drive on the system of life is to affirm, whatever spiritual questions remain unsolved, a meaning in existence that transcends existence, a coherence that begins in the unconquerable self. In our own time, viewed calmly against a long background of existential inquiry, such a response is nearly commonplace. In the spiritually troubled world portrayed in the *Life*, the same response is nearly Promethean.

Along with this theme of personal heroism there runs, throughout Boswell's description of the final period, a public or cultural symbolism associated with Johnson's passing. The last part of the *Life* contains a displaced version of what we conventionally identify as the elegiac mood—a sense that, with the death of the hero, an age is coming to an end. When we think of the occurrence of this mood in heroic literature, the scenes that come to mind will be, as with the death of Beowulf or Roland or the passing of Arthur in Malory or Tennyson, those in which some idealized social order dissolves: a *comitatus* relationship, a fellowship of the Round Table. In the *Life* we are dealing with a world of private coherence sustained by Johnson's majestic presence, a sphere in which lesser men move reassured. This, though on one level a world of people and places, is also a moral order, a projection of Johnson's heroic mind and will.

This projection has been, throughout the *Life*, symbolically extensive. We think, for instance, of the topographical symbolism which identifies Johnson so strongly with London or which creates the pastoral mood associated with his annual jaunts into the countryside. In the final period this identification of the landscape with certain phases of the hero's existence incorporates the pathos of a dying man visiting familiar scenes for the last time; the effect is to enlarge our anticipation of the cultural impact of the hero's death. We have Johnson, temporarily recovered from a severe illness, visiting Oxford for the last time: "he bore the journey very well, and seemed to feel himself elevated

as he approached Oxford, that magnificent and venerable seat
of Learning, Orthodoxy, and Toryism" (IV.284–85). Or Johnson at Lichfield, fighting intellectual boredom even in his last
days: "such was his love of London, so high a relish had he of its
magnificent extent, and variety of intellectual entertainment, that
he languished when absent from it . . . and, therefore, although at
Lichfield, surrounded with friends who loved and revered him
. . . he still found that such conversation as London affords, could
be found nowhere else" (IV.374–75).

Just before Johnson's death, our sense of what is normally
called the hero's "world" is heightened, made more vivid and
concrete; at his passing, the sense of projected personal identity
that held these scenes together and gave them emotional meaning will be gone. It is this implication of momentous loss that
underlies the elegiac mood. At the end we have the sense of a
fulfilled decorum when Boswell falls into something like an epic
tone in approaching the grand event. Though the last part of
the *Life* has pursued a story of near-despair and continuous physical suffering, the heroic dimension has been sustained, and Boswell's tone at the end seems only its logical culmination: "my
readers are now, at last, to behold SAMUEL JOHNSON preparing
himself for that doom, from which the most exalted powers afford
not exemption to man" (IV.394); "it is not my intention to give
a very minute detail of the particulars of Johnson's remaining
days, of whom it was now evident, that the crisis was fast approaching, when he must '*die like men, and fall like one of the
Princes*' " (IV.398–99).

At the last, all sense of personal loss giving way to the grander
impersonality of the elegiac mood, Boswell leaves the concluding utterance to an anonymous spokesman for the age which
Johnson has dominated: " 'he has made a chasm, which not only
nothing can fill up, but which nothing has a tendency to fill
up.—Johnson is dead.—Let us go to the next best:—There
is nobody; no man can be said to put you in mind of Johnson' "

(IV.420–21). Yet there is a sadness about Johnson's death that lies beyond the reach of elegy and that has all along been inseparable from Boswell's conception of the hero. In the image of a chasm, a vacuum, a world without a center, there is a formal and conventional truth, one appropriate to a time when the passing of a superior man be taken to symbolize the passing of an age. Yet the full meaning of Boswellian narrative lies beyond this conventional truth, for Boswell has given us the image of a world that cannot survive its hero, a separate world of moral stability in the midst of moral chaos, born out of a heroic conflict with the age.

EPILOGUE

An interpretation of the theme of the hero in Boswell, in returning to the notion of literary autonomy from which it began, suggests certain theoretical conclusions that have remained implicit in our argument. For what is involved in such an interpretation is a distinction sometimes ignored in literary studies, the distinction between literary and critical theory. So far as it involves a theory of biography as a genre, and so far as that theory involves a larger theory of literature as an order of symbolic meaning, our interpretation is an exercise in literary theory, or theory of literature. The theory *that* literature represents an autonomous order of meaning, on the other hand, is a critical theory, or theory of interpretation, that underlies and controls—in the fullest sense actually creates—the mode of interpretation employed.

The most essential issue involved when we speak of the autonomy of biography is the logic of objective interpretation, or interpretation conceived as a universe of discourse with literature as its object of inquiry. As the theory of autonomy, so far as it is genuinely a theory, is now generally viewed as the legacy of the intrinsic or formalist approach that dominated literary studies some twenty years ago, we may very briefly review one important episode in the story: the movement that began with Warren and Wellek's *Theory of Literature* (1947), gained momentum with Wimsatt and Beardsley's *The Verbal Icon* (1954), and moved into an entirely new stage with Northrop Frye's *Anatomy of Criticism* (1957).

When we recall the controversy surrounding the movement

toward intrinsic interpretation now, what comes most readily to mind is the endless argument over such matters as authorial intention and affective response—and, in the years following the appearance of the *Anatomy of Criticism*, over the issue of whether evaluation has any legitimate role in literary study. Yet what remains significant about the movement is the single vision that animated the formalist theorists. To argue that a literary work exists independent of its author's intentions and the responses of its readers or that evaluation is an empty expression of cultural anxieties was to argue ultimately that literature composes a permanent and universal order of meaning comprehensible only in its own terms. This is the vision of literature that retains so powerful an influence in modern literary study.

At the same time, it can be argued that the theory of literary autonomy developed by the formalist theorists was never a genuine theory, that it was in reality an attempt to explain—through such concepts as autonomy and such metaphors as "closed form"—the results of an objective *method* introduced into literary study for the first time. For the notion of literary autonomy is as old as Aristotle's *Poetics,* and it runs through the history of English criticism from Sir Philip Sidney to Shelley's *Defense of Poetry* to the aesthetic theories of Oscar Wilde. The revolutionary element in formalist theory was not theoretical: it was the development of an interpretive method that may be traced back to such works as I. A. Richard's *Practical Criticism*. This is the context in which a study like Cleanth Brooks's *The Well-Wrought Urn*, a work largely of interpretation rather than theory, was as important to the movement as the great theoretical work of Wellek or Wimsatt.

It is also possible to argue that the theory of autonomy as advanced by formalist theorists created as many problems as it solved, and even that the theory, as an unsatisfactory attempt to justify a method that needed no justification, was responsible for its own demise. It is with a certain sense of the ludicrous that we look back today on the crude metaphor of the literary work as a "closed form," a sort of physical object or vessel of meaning occupying a place in three-dimensional space. Yet it was just this metaphor that impelled critical theorists, all of them intelligent and all of them otherwise expert in the interpretation of literary metaphor, to discuss endlessly what lay "inside" and "outside" the literary work. It is precisely to the degree that the formalists' theory of autonomy depended on such unsatisfactory metaphors that it never constituted a genuine theory.

In one sense, then, the notion of autonomy advanced in formalist theory has never been generally accepted or rejected. For what was rejected was not the theory of autonomy but the metaphors with which it was justified, and even these were not in any true sense rejected. What occurred instead was something less dramatic: in the debate over autonomy, such metaphors as closed form gradually revealed their insufficiency, and after a time died the quiet and unregarded death reserved for metaphors posing as axioms. Yet their retirement from the theoretical arena was not without important consequences, for what followed was a period of exhaustion in theory, a climate in which the attempt to construct a coherent theoretical account of interpretive principles would either run in circles over fallow ground or cease altogether in favor of practical interpretation. This is to a very real extent the climate in which we operate today.

In just the same sense, the theory of autonomy was never accepted. What earned a general acceptance was the method of objective interpretation that the notion of autonomy was meant to explain and justify, the method employed in this study and in most studies in modern literary interpretation. To observe that the method needs no justification is not, in the context of literary studies now, to attempt any grand gesture of avoidance: it is simply to acknowledge that in the annals of objective knowledge method has always preceded theory of method. In the history of science, mainly because scientific method was the earliest mode of objective inquiry, this is a wholly familiar story: the physicist working after the appearance of Newton's *Principia* needed no theory of experimentation to perform his experiments— he needed only what T. H. Kuhn refers to as the paradigm of the Newtonian universe—and a theory of the physicist's theory has only recently become the concern of philosophers of science. This is the story now repeating itself, within a shorter compass of time, in such disciplines as psychology, history, and literary studies.

At the same time, our attempt to interpret the meaning of such works as the *Tour to Corsica* and the *Life of Johnson* in purely internal terms—the metaphor dies unwillingly—seems to demand explanation in light of some theory of objective inter- pretation. The theory implicit in this study involves no very radical adjustment of the terms inherited from formalist theo- rists. When we have abandoned their metaphors we are left with all that is really essential to any coherent explanation of interpretation as objective knowledge: the objective method, with a logic composed of rules of inference and hypothesis, and that which we call "literature," the state of affairs interpretation exists to elucidate. The relation between the two implies some- thing like a complete theory of objective interpretation.

An epilogue to a study of the hero in Boswell is not the place to undertake an analysis of the rules of inference and hypothesis governing objective interpretation, yet the conclusions suggested by such an analysis may be briefly set out. In approaching the *Life of Johnson* as a work of literature we consciously or un- consciously enter a methodological universe in which literature is a state of affairs mirrored in propositions about literary mean- ing, and in doing so we in a manner of speaking *create* the autonomy for which the metaphors of formalist theory attempted to account. For "literature" in relation to objective interpreta- tion exists, like "nature" in relation to physics or "history" in relation to historical explanation, as a state of affairs created by its universe of discourse. The theory of objective inquiry derives, in short, from one essential insight: just as no interpretation can exist independent of an object of inquiry, no object of inquiry can exist independent of some mode of interpretation.

The danger of expressing the insight in these terms is that it may seem either self-evident or merely circular. Yet what follows from so simple an observation is that objective interpretation creates literature as a state of affairs, in just the same way as the universe of discourse we call physics creates, through its rules of inference and hypothesis, the state of affairs mirrored in the propositions of physics. (We may be tempted to call this state of affairs the "physical universe," but it bears little relation to the physical universe inhabited by the non-physicist.) A corollary principle need only be mentioned: a state of affairs, once constituted as an object of inquiry, controls its mode of interpretation—this is why the methods of the psychologist will not serve to explain the behavior of the electron, the methods of the physicist to explain the events leading up to the French Revolution.

Only one implication of this theory of objective inquiry need concern us here, though it is something close to an ultimate implication: if we count ordinary discourse only as one mode of interpretation among others, the phenomenal world in objective terms dissolves into states of affairs, none "real" except in relation to the universe of discourse in whose logic it is mirrored, none prior or antecedent to any other. This, within the narrower sphere of literary studies, is what the theory of autonomy attempted to account for: just as the rottenness of the apple has no existence in physics—or its redness or even its appleness (it could be a falling pear)—an entire range of data belonging to other universes of discourse (the author's intention, the reader's response, evidence for the existence of an historical Samuel Johnson) has no meaning in objective literary interpretation.

As the objective method of interpretation resolves the problem of biography, then, a theory of objective inquiry reveals the sense in which any assumed categoric distinction between imaginative and factual literature constitutes a pseudo problem. For we are not dealing with categories but with states of affairs: the reader who uses the *Life of Johnson* as a source of evidence about a "real" Samuel Johnson exists and thinks within a different universe of discourse from the reader who perceives the *Life* as a work of literature, and each is occupied with a separate object of inquiry. The notion of conflict between the two modes of perception and interpretation— each equally coherent and objective in its own terms—arises only when we have no notion of what it means to move from one universe of discourse to another.

The real problem of imaginative versus factual literature derives, then, from a mistaken tendency to think of a work like the *Life of Johnson* as an object-in-itself existing independent of any universe of discourse whatever. Yet the object-in-itself does not exist, and there is no conflict between or among objects of inquiry: where the physicist sees an endless whirl of electrons and the botanist sees a system of respiration and photosynthesis, the ordinary man sees a tree; and all are right, and each—when he once knows how—can see as the others see. The *Life of Johnson* is not one object but two or three or many, as many as there are universes of discourse in which it contains phenomena to be explained. The argument for the literary autonomy of biography and of "factual" literature generally reduces in the end to this: in any other universe of discourse the *Life* is in a secondary relation to some object of inquiry not identical with itself, while in literary interpretation it is itself the sole object of inquiry.

The claims of objective interpretation are not likely to be resisted in modern literary studies. The argument about the role of the hero in Boswell set forth in this study will be judged in its own terms, and these are just the terms in which an interpretation of *King Lear* or *Bleak House* would be judged sound or unsound. Indeed, the challenge to its theoretical principles comes now not from the central movement in literary studies but from the varieties of antiinterpretation—the oracular psychohistory of Harold Bloom, the empty affectivism of Stanley Fish, the "deconstructivist" criticism that is the latest continental importation of J. Hillis Miller—that have emerged to fill the theoretical vacuum created by the demise of formalist theory. Yet that challenge is to all works of objective interpretation equally and will persist only until a coherent theory of objective method is worked out.

For literary studies generally, the more significant problem is one that since Aristotle's *Poetics* has been associated with a notion of the universality of literary meaning, a perception of literature as composing a permanent and timeless order in relation to ordinary life as, in Pater's words, "the concurrence, renewed from moment to moment, of forces parting sooner or later on their ways." This is what Aristotle had in mind when he described poetry as being a higher and more philosophical thing than history, what Sidney had in mind when he said that art gives us a golden world and nature only a brazen one, what Shelley meant when he spoke of poets as the unacknowledged legislators of mankind. It is the vision that informs Oscar Wilde's description of the *Iliad* as a timeless reality: "heroes of mist and mountain? Shadows in a song? No: they are real. Action! What is action? It dies at the moment of its energy. It is a base concession to fact. The world is made by the singer for the dreamer."

If we take the aesthetic doctrines of Wilde only as an extreme expression of a perception of literature going back to ancient Greece—and if we see such works as Plutarch's *Lives* and Boswell's *Life of Johnson* as belonging to the same realm as the *Iliad* and the *Odyssey*—we are compelled to account in modern terms for the persistence of this idea of universality. And the need to do so is rendered more compelling precisely because the objective method employed in modern literary studies insists, though in a different way, on just this notion of universal meaning: to take literature as an object of inquiry is no other than to recognize its existence as a permanent and timeless realm of meaning. This too is what the theory of literary autonomy aimed to explain and justify, and the problem remains unresolved.

The solution lies, we may suspect, in the nature of objective comprehension itself, and to see the problem in its true light we must begin and end by abandoning any notion of ordinary experience as a mode of perception existing prior to all others. The great truth of Nabokov's remark that "real" is the only word in the language that is meaningless unless placed in quotation marks is finally an epistemological truth. Our tendency to say that the "real" tree dissolves into the whirling electrons of the physicist means no more than that the majority of us inhabit a reality in which trees are growing things with leaves and twigs and branches rather than a colorless dance of elementary particles. And even the physicist, when he removes his laboratory coat and walks to his automobile, enters the same world as the rest of us. The realm of ordinary experience remains real only through epistemological consensus.

Yet when we attempt to explain why any such realm as literature or music or mathematics or logic seems to possess a separate and autonomous existence, we are very close to perceiving that the consensus is, in its claim to be prior to every other form of knowledge, an arbitrary fiction. For to read *King Lear* or listen to a Beethoven symphony or comprehend Gödel's theorum is to perform an act of objective comprehension, and the essence of objective comprehension is to annihilate all other worlds—including the world of ordinary experience—outside itself. In any moment of literary comprehension it is only literature that is real, and the ordinary world exists only as a grand unarticulated analogue of that reality.

A perception of literature as possessing a universal significance implies nothing less than an awareness that ordinary experience enjoys no primacy in the order of knowing, that the objective comprehension of literary meaning dissolves the epistemological consensus from which the dream of an ordinary world derives. For what is universal in literature is that it exists as a state of affairs on which all acts of objective literary comprehension must converge, and what is annihilated in the moment of comprehension is not the ordinary world but the fragmentary perceptions of the ordinary world existing separately in separate minds. It is not literature that is universal in this sense but the entire realm of objective knowledge existing apart from any individual mind.

Yet literature will always remain a very great part of this possession, and an objective approach to biography needs no other justification than that it makes accessible to us a rich and unexplored portion of the realm. Beyond all theoretical reasoning lies the literary reality of the works composing the biographical tradition in narrative and the experience of opening such a work as the *Life of Johnson* to return to a world—"Boswell, *lend* me sixpence, *not* to be repaid"—as permanent and timeless as the worlds of Shakespeare and Homer. The heroes of Boswellian narrative, we may say with Wilde, are neither heroes of mist and mountain nor shadows in a song. They are, like Achilles and Hector, real.

NOTES

Passages from the *Tour to Corsica* are taken from the text included in *Boswell on the Grand Tour: Italy, Corsica, and France*, ed. Frank Brady and F. A. Pottle (London: Heinemann, 1955). Passages from the *Tour to the Hebrides* and the *Life of Johnson* are from the Hill-Powell edition: *The Life of Johnson*, ed. G. B. Hill, rev. L. F. Powell, 6 vols. (Oxford: Oxford University Press, 1934–1964). Volume and page numbers are cited parenthetically.

The notes that follow should be regarded as notes to an essay: isolated phrases from well-known writers have not been footnoted, nor have longer passages from works—e.g., Carlyle's *Heroes and Hero-Worship*, Walton's *Lives*—which exist in numerous editions and which may be assumed to be familiar to the scholarly reader.

PREFACE

1. Scott's argument, which originally appeared in vol. 6 of the privately printed Isham edition, now appears more accessibly in "The Making of *The Life of Johnson* as shown in Boswell's First Notes," in *Twentieth Century Interpretations of Boswell's Life of Johnson*, ed. James L. Clifford (Englewood Cliffs, N.J.: Prentice-Hall, 1970). The passage quoted is on page 33 of this volume.

2. Frederick A. Pottle, ed., intro. to *Boswell's London Journal, 1762–1763* (New York: McGraw-Hill, 1950), p. 12.

3. In *Hateful Contraries* (Lexington: University of Kentucky Press, 1965), p. 183.

4. Frank Brady, ed., intro. to *Boswell's Life of Johnson* (New York: Signet, 1968), p. 11.

5. Ralph W. Rader, "Literary Form in Factual Narrative: The Example of Boswell's *Johnson*," in *Essays in Eighteenth-Century Biography*, ed. Philip B. Daghlian (Bloomington: Indiana University Press, 1968), p. 4.

INTRODUCTION

1. Geoffrey Scott, "The Making of *The Life of Johnson*," p. 38.

2. Cf. Frank Brady's fine commentary on the implications of this passage: "Boswell's central thematic purpose is to construct an epic, a moral epic of heroic proportions, in which a man with greater strengths and weaknesses than ordinary, struggles with the problems of daily life and overcomes them. The remote model for that epic is the *Odyssey* with its archetypal journey pattern, the *Life* substituting a journey in time for one in space. . . . Of all the versions of epic produced in the eighteenth century—*The Rape of the Lock*, *The Dunciad*, *Tom Jones*, *The Decline and Fall of the Roman Empire*, even Blake's major prophecies—Boswell's remains the most immediate to our everyday concerns." "The Strategies of Biography and Some Eighteenth-Century Examples," in *Literary Theory and Structure: Essays in Honor of William K. Wimsatt*, ed. Frank Brady, John Palmer, and Martin Price (New Haven: Yale University Press, 1973), p. 256.

3. Northrop Frye, *Anatomy of Criticism* (Princeton: Princeton University Press, 1957), p. 34.

4. Thomas Edwards, *Imagination and Power* (New York: Oxford University Press, 1971), p. 8.

5. Robert Scholes and Robert Kellogg, *The Nature of Narrative* (Oxford: Oxford University Press, 1966), p. 36.

6. Walter E. Houghton, *The Victorian Frame of Mind* (New Haven: Yale University Press, 1957), p. 71.

7. John Morley, *On Compromise*, quoted in Houghton, pp. 66–67.

8. Bertrand H. Bronson, *Johnson Agonistes and Other Essays* (Cambridge: Cambridge University Press, 1946), p. 44.

9. The phrase is from Edward Bulwer Lytton's *England and the English*.

10. David L. Passler, *Time, Form, and Style in Boswell's Life of Johnson* (New Haven: Yale University Press, 1971), p. 74.

CHAPTER ONE

1. *Boswelliana, the Commonplace Book of James Boswell*, ed. Charles Rogers (1874), p. 328.

2. Frederick A. Pottle, *James Boswell: The Earlier Years, 1740–1769* (New York: McGraw-Hill, 1966), p. 367.

3. Quoted in Chauncey Brewster Tinker, *Nature's Simple Plan* (Princeton: Princeton University Press, 1922), pp. 38, 54.

4. Pottle, *The Earlier Years*, p. 248.

5. Tinker, p. 34.

6. Pottle, *The Earlier Years*, p. 248.

7. Tinker, pp. 36–37.

8. William R. Siebenschuh, *Form and Purpose in Boswell's Biographical Works* (Berkeley, Los Angeles, and London: University of California Press, 1972), p. 71.

9. Quoted in Tinker, p. 39.

10. Cf. F. A. Pottle's remarks on the difference in reaction to the *Life of Johnson* and the *Tour to Corsica*: "some intelligent and sensitive readers hate Boswell's Johnson at first sight and on further acquaintance are only confirmed in their dislike. . . . The Plutarchian *Journal of a Tour to Corsica* produced no such double reaction. It would be possible to collect pages and pages of contemporary comment to prove this, but Wesley's record will suffice. The reading public felt for Paoli (whom they knew *solely* through Boswell's book) a pitch of veneration for which their own term might have been 'enthusiastic' " (*The Earlier Years*, pp. 363–64).

CHAPTER TWO

1. Johnsonophilus, "Johnsoniana, from Boswell's *Journey*, with Remarks," *Gentleman's Magazine* (December 1785), p. 967.

2. Brady, "The Strategies of Biography," p. 260.

3. Passler, *Time, Form, and Style*, p. 142.

CHAPTER THREE

1. Gray made these remarks in a letter to Horace Walpole, 25 February 1768. See *Horace Walpole's Correspondence*, ed. W. S. Lewis and others (New Haven, 1937–), 14:174.

2. (Cambridge: Harvard University Press, 1971), pp. 24–25.

3. Intro. to *The Hero in Literature*, ed. Victor Brombert (Greenwich, Conn.: Fawcett Publications, 1969), p. 11.

4. Thomas Edwards, *Imagination and Power* (New York: Oxford University Press, 1971), p. 9.

5. Quoted in Joseph W. Reed, *English Biography in the Early*

Nineteenth Century (New Haven: Yale University Press, 1966), p. 6.

6. "Boswell's Control of Aesthetic Distance," *University of Toronto Quarterly* 38 (1969):174–91.

7. In "Boswell's Self-Presentation and his Critics," *Studies in English Literature* 12 (1972):545–55, Brady specifically describes Boswell as an *ingénu.*

8. Brady, "The Strategies of Biography," p. 262.

9. Bronson, *Johnson Agonistes*, p. 76.

CHAPTER FOUR

1. Jeffrey Hart, ed., intro. to *Political Writers of Eighteenth-Century England*, (New York: Knopf, 1964), p. 5.

2. Quoted in Houghton, p. 68.

3. Quoted in Houghton, p. 332.

4. Brombert, intro. to *The Hero in Literature*, p. 12.

5. The dynamics of this scene, with which I have only partially dealt, are acutely discussed by Michael Rewa, "Biography as an Imitative Art," *English Symposium Papers* (Fredonia, N.Y., 1970), pp. 18–19.

6. Quoted in Houghton, p. 73.

7. Thomas McFarland, *Tragic Meanings in Shakespeare* (New York: Random House, 1966), p. 11.

8. Peter Gay, *The Enlightenment: An Interpretation*, 2 vols. (New York: Knopf, 1966, 1969), 2:86.

BIBLIOGRAPHICAL NOTE

Though literature on the theme of the hero in Boswell is virtually nonexistent, this study owes much to general studies of Boswell and his writings and even more to the modern scholarship that makes interpretive study of Boswell a possibility. Such works as bear directly on my own argument are cited in the notes, but a few words may be said about their relative importance in Boswellian studies as a whole and also about several titles not cited.

The theoretical background of the study will be obvious to readers who have taken an interest in contemporary theory. I first began thinking about an objective or internal approach to biography when, early in college, I read W. K. Wimsatt's *The Verbal Icon* (Lexington: University of Kentucky Press, 1954). The arguments for literary autonomy advanced in that great work were (and remain) a profound influence on my approach to biography and to literature as a whole. Similarly I regard Northrop Frye's *Anatomy of Criticism* (Princeton: Princeton University Press, 1957) as the completion of the first stage of the objective program in modern interpretation, and its influence is everywhere present in this study. More recently my thinking about objective interpretation has been influenced by Karl R. Popper's *Objective Knowledge* (Oxford: Oxford University Press, 1970) and I. M. Bochenski's *The Methods of Contemporary Thought* (trans. Peter Caws, Dordrecht, Holland: D. Reidel, 1965).

Any interpretive study of Boswell's writings undertaken today stands on awesome foundations: in few areas of literary study has scholarship been so thorough, so original, or so complete. I need only mention the great Hill-Powell edition of the *Life of Johnson* and the editions of Boswell's journals issued by Yale and McGraw-Hill. In the early stages of my research I had frequent recourse as well to the privately printed volumes of the Malahide Edition: *The Private Papers of James Boswell from Malahide Castle in the Collection of Lieutenant Colonel Ralph Heyward Isham*, 18 vols., ed. Geoffrey Scott and Frederick A. Pottle (Mt. Vernon, N.Y., 1928–1934).

I may mention, too, several other works that have been my constant companions during the writing of *The Boswellian Hero*. Though all references in the text are to the Hill-Powell edition of the *Tour to the Hebrides* (the work known to Boswell's contemporary readers), I have very often consulted the edition taken by Frederick A. Pottle and Charles H. Bennett from the original manuscript and published by McGraw-Hill in 1961. Another work indispensible to my research has been the Yale edition of materials relating to the *Life of Johnson*, superbly edited by Marshall Waingrow: *The Correspondence and Other Papers of James Boswell Relating to the Life of Johnson* (New York: McGraw-Hill, 1970). My chapter on the *Tour to Corsica* owes a debt, in its background, to Joseph Foldare's Yale dissertation, "James Boswell and Corsica" (1936). Finally, I have constantly consulted F. A. Pottle's *The Literary Career of James Boswell* (Oxford: Oxford University Press, 1929), surely the model of what a bibliographical study ought to be.

An argument can be made that without the lifelong and inspired researches of Professor Pottle there would be no modern Boswell studies. At any rate, his *James Boswell: The Early Years* (New York: McGraw-Hill, 1966) is as fine an introduction to Boswell's life and work as could be imagined. Though much narrower in focus, Frank Brady's *Boswell's Political Career* (New Haven: Yale University Press, 1965) is a valuable supplementary study that sheds important light on Boswell's career as a writer.

Interpretive study of Boswell's works, on the other hand, has just begun. David L. Passler's *Time, Form, and Style in Boswell's Life of Johnson* (New Haven: Yale University Press, 1971) attempts, sometimes usefully, to deal with the thematic structure of Boswell's major work, and William R. Siebenschuh's *Form and Purpose in Boswell's Biographical Works* (Berkeley: University of California Press, 1972) is useful, for readers previously unacquainted with the work, for commentary on the *Tour to Corsica*.

Of the articles cited in the notes, several stand out as having broken new ground in the interpretive study of Boswell. W. K. Wimsatt's "The Fact Imagined" was and remains a classic attempt to direct discourse about Boswell into literary channels. Frank Brady's "The Strategies of Biography and Some Eighteenth-Century Examples" offers a finely considered treatment of the *Life of Johnson* against its literary background. Paul Alkon's "Boswell's Control of Aesthetic Distance," an immensely suggestive treatment of the *Life of Johnson*, contains many insights that yet remain to be pursued in Boswell studies. Ralph W. Rader's "Literary Form and Factual Narrative," though I regard its argument as being unfortunate on theoretical grounds, contains sound and sensitive treatment of several important scenes in the *Life*.

Several essays not cited in the course of my argument should also be mentioned. Sven Eric Molin's "Boswell's Account of the Johnson-Wilkes Meeting" (*Studies in English Literature* 3 [1963]: 307–22) was a groundbreaking attempt to explain one aspect of the literary structure of the *Life of Johnson*. More recently Felicity Nussbaum's "Boswell's Treatment of Johnson's Temper" (*Studies in English Literature* 14 [1974]: 421–33), does the same. Robert H. Bell's "Boswell's Notes towards a Supreme Fiction" (*Modern Language Quarterly* 38 [1977]: 132–48) offers a superb treatment of Boswell's change in narrative posture between the *London Journal* and the *Life of Johnson*. Ronald Primeau's "Boswell's 'Romantic Imagination' in the *London Journal*" (*Papers on Language and Literature* 9 [1973]: 15–27) contains some sensible remarks on the *Life of Johnson*. And Paul Alkon's "Boswellian Time" (*Studies in Burke and His Time* 14 [1973]: 239–56) should be read, in its subtlety and suggestiveness, as a companion piece to his previously mentioned essay on aesthetic distance.

The theoretical ground on which this study stands makes the substantial body of literature on Samuel Johnson, generally of so high a quality, irrelevant to its concerns, for that literature deals almost exclusively with Johnson as man and writer and not as literary protagonist and Boswellian hero. (It must be said that when Johnson scholars do write about Boswell their viewpoint too often derives—as in the hectoring anti-Boswellianism of Donald J. Greene—from a simple failure or inability to read works like the *Life of Johnson* as literature.) Yet I must mention two classic studies that influenced me in the early stages of this work: Bertrand H. Bronson's "Johnson Agonistes" (in *Johnson Agonistes and Other Essays*, Cambridge: Cambridge University Press, 1946), and Walter Jackson Bate's *The Achievement of Samuel Johnson* (Oxford: Oxford University Press, 1955). Neither is about Boswell's Johnson, yet both remain immensely suggestive for serious students of Boswell.

For readers interested in the larger body of scholarship and commentary surrounding Boswell's life and writings, a useful general bibliography is Anthony E. Brown's *Boswellian Studies* (Hamden, Conn.: Archon Books, 1972). Brown's bibliography should be supplemented for works published after 1971 by consulting *The Eigh-teenth Century: A Current Bibliography*, included annually until 1975 in *Philological Quarterly*, issued thereafter each year by the American Society for Eighteenth-Century Studies.

INDEX

THE AUTHOR

William C. Dowling is assistant professor of English at the University of New Mexico. He is the author of *The Critic's Hornbook*, an introduction to literary interpretation, and of articles published in *Critical Inquiry*, *Studies in English Literature*, *Studies in Scottish Literature*, and *Harvard English Studies*.